THE ECONOMICS
OF PUBLIC ISSUES

DOUGLASS C. NORTH
ROGER LEROY MILLER
University of Washington

The Economics
of Public Issues

Harper & Row, Publishers
New York / Evanston / San Francisco / London

THE ECONOMICS
OF PUBLIC ISSUES

Copyright © 1971 by Douglass C. North and Roger LeRoy Miller

Standard Book Number: 06-044858-X

Library of Congress Catalog Card Number: 70-151995

This book is about some issues of our time. In it we attempt to show what economics can contribute to the analysis and to possible solutions to these issues. No a priori knowledge of economics is necessary for understanding the articles. The reader is warned that in no case is our treatment of a topic exhaustive. We have merely attempted to expose the bare economic bones of some aspects of the issues treated. From there further discussion should be possible. We suggest that the chapters be read in order, since later chapters usually build upon earlier discussions.

When economic concepts are first introduced, we have tried, with some consistency, to italicize them. Many times we have inserted the more technical terminology in parenthesis.

For professors using this book we have prepared a short *Instructor's Manual* which we think is useful. It is available to instructors upon request from the publisher.

Economists cannot tell people what they ought to do. They can only expose the costs and benefits of various alternatives so that the citizens in a democratic society can make better choices. That is the purpose of this book.

415157

Several of our colleagues read the manuscript in its incipient stages. We wish to thank Judith Cox, John Allan
Hynes and John McGee of the University of Washington for
all of their critical comments. Also, we especially wish to
thank Robert J. Lampman for his remarks and for pointing
out some important lacunas which we hope we eliminated
to some degree. Mrs. Marion Dunsmore helped with edit-
ing. We also wish to thank Susan Vita Miller for the count-
less hours she spent helping us and Marijane Anderson for
typing some preliminary drafts. All errors remaining are of
course our sole responsibility.

Douglass C. North
Roger LeRoy Miller

CONTENTS

THE ECONOMICS
OF PUBLIC ISSUES

1
THE ECONOMICS
OF THE POPULATION
"CRISIS"

People may not reproduce like rabbits, nor even in the geometric ratios which Thomas Malthus, that dismal forecaster, conjectured. But historically, the number of the world's inhabitants has tended to outstrip the available food supply. And when those numbers have pressed too hard on available resources, either famine or pestilence has succeeded in decimating man's ranks. That, at least, has been the case until modern times. During the past 200 years the situation has changed, especially in those parts of the Western world where man has climbed to an unprecedented standard of abundance. More surprisingly, this change has been achieved during a period of phenomenal population growth. The world held a population of roughly 730 million inhabitants in 1750 and of more than 2.5 billion a century later. Now, more than 4 billion humans walk this planet. Have we, nonetheless, finally emerged into permanent abundance, or is this merely a Utopian interlude, at least in the United States?

The easiest way to understand this issue is first to look at the centuries prior to 1750, and then to compare the situation of the modern world. During the centuries of chaos that followed the decline and fall of the Roman Empire, the number of people in Western Europe appears to have decreased. Then, from approximately the ninth century until the end of the thirteenth, population grew in that region. Another reversal came in the fourteenth century, beginning with a severe famine between 1315 and 1317 and compounded by the nightmare of the Black Death which swept over Europe for the first time between 1347 and 1351. The plague became endemic to the Occident, raging again and again in the next century, so that population declined absolutely for at least a century. Then another cycle of growth set in (about 1470–1580) followed by at least stagnation (1580–1680). Since then, population has grown continuously, although the rate did not begin to accelerate until the last half of the eighteenth century.

This growth pattern can probably be explained by the same factors which for many millennia must have determined the number of inhabitants on the earth. The crucial and interrelated elements are: (a) the size of population; (b) the techniques (tools, equipment, knowledge) which man has at his command; and (c) the land and resources available to him. Man's technical knowledge grew relatively slowly during the first 1,700 years after Christ. If we look at the population of Western Europe in the ninth century in relation to the land available, it is evident that vast parts of Northwestern Europe were sparsely settled or even in a state of absolute wilderness. As population grew in particularly favored areas, the amount of land per man of course decreased, and not even the additional labor available could maintain the previous per capita supply of food. But that was no cause for concern, since anyone who felt crowded or deprived could simply move out to the unsettled frontiers. On this basis, colonization of Western Europe continued for centuries. Even lacking any improvement in technical knowledge, the additional population could produce as much as their predecessors because of the abundance of rich virgin land. During this period, therefore, the output of foodstuffs, as well as of materials for clothing, housing, and other necessities, at least held at a constant amount per capita.

There came a time when this situation changed. By about 1180 all the best land in Western Europe had been taken up, and *constant returns* gave way to *diminishing returns*. An additional peasant now had either to work the existing cultivated agricultural land more intensively than before or to move onto what proved to be poorer land. In either case the amount of foodstuffs (and other raw materials) that he could produce was less than that of his predecessors. Between 1180 and 1300 the continued growth of population resulted generally in diminishing returns (to additional labor effort) and a progressive fall in the standard of life of the peasant. Weakened by malnutrition, he was an easy prey first to famine and then to pestilence. Once the latter had become embedded in the environment, it continued to make inroads long after the populace had declined to levels that left a good deal of excellent land vacant.

Whether the plague gradually petered out or the surviving peasantry built up some degree of immunity to it, population began to grow again. A second cycle of growth and diminishing returns occurred between 1450 and 1680. But there was a difference which made the second decline far less deadly. Not only had migration to the New World become possible, but new techniques at man's command aided him in producing more per individual than before.

Continuing to our own day, it is technical and organizational progress which has permitted output to grow so dramatically in the past two centuries as to pace the astronomical increase in population. In effect, improvements in machinery, power, fertilizer, and seed have made it possible for man to wring ever-higher yields from a given acre of land. Comparable improvements in efficiency have occurred in nonagricultural activities.

To the present, this increase in man's productivity has outstripped the growth of population in many countries. Whether it can continue to do so depends on: (a) whether man can discover technologies to overcome diminishing returns, (b) whether the side effects of man's exploitation of the environment will destroy him, and (c) changing fertility and mortality rates. Let us examine these last factors.

The rate of population growth is a function of the rates of birth and death. While both have responded to economic changes, the triumphant decline of mortality in the past two centuries accounted for much of the population growth. Anyone who thinks of the modern city as polluted would be appalled by the unsanitary conditions of its counterpart of even a century ago. When rising living standards were coupled with the application of improved sanitary and medical knowledge, the decline in death rates, particularly among infants, became a potent factor in population levels.

However, it is not to the mortality rate but to the birth rate that civilized man must turn for control of population size. Fertility has responded in some degree to economic conditions even before modern contraceptives were devised. In earlier centuries, periods of famine and declining income were countered by delaying the age of marriage and by primitive forms of birth control (sometimes even by infanticide). However, with the development of modern and efficient forms of contraception and the widespread practice of illegal or legal abortion, fertility (or lack of it) has become a deliberate decision for many. At least in developed countries, whether to have children and how many to have, are regarded as decisions to be arrived at by rational choice on the part of the family unit.

In the agricultural world of the past centuries, children were, for their parents, as much an investment as a source of enjoyment. On the farm a child could probably "pay his way" by age eight, and the family farm essentially recruited its labor force from within. Moreover, since children were counted on to care for aging parents, an "extended family system" served as a form of social security. As we would expect, therefore, fertility rates in agricultural societies were high. In the United States until very recently, farm families were much larger than city families, and in developing nations large families are considered an economic safeguard.

Why do urban couples have children? They are certainly not a good investment economically. From birth they require large expenditures on which no "returns" of gratitude, much less of income, can be confidently anticipated. Parents have children for their own enjoyment. That is to say, in economic terms, that children are a consumption rather than an investment good; moreover, the economic costs of this consumption good have been rising substantially. The Institute of Life Insurance has estimated that the median-income family must spend $30,000 raising one child until age eighteen. Since parents usually support their children throughout their years of schooling, for the most part, and since the costs of education have been rising relative to other goods and services, children have been growing relatively more expensive. We would expect, therefore, in the absence of a change in people's tastes in favor of children rather than other consumption goods, that fertility would decline as an ever-growing portion of Americans becomes urbanized and is faced with the rising cost of raising and educating children. And that is precisely what is happening. Fertility among whites is at one of the lowest levels in our history; if the present trend continues, the white population will have a zero rate of population increase in another decade or two.

It appears that economic considerations do indeed affect fertility rates. If that is correct, and we wish to use these incentives to reduce fertility, then we should keep in mind that proposals to establish family allotments according to the number of children (as provided in some countries) would appear likely to increase fertility. Even the modest deduction of $600 per child permitted under our present federal tax law acts in that direction, for that matter.

If we truly wish to reduce birth rates, the means are at hand. They would take the form of dissuasive tax incentives —that is, tax rates increasing with the number of children. We are not suggesting that this is the only course of action, or an appropriate one. It is merely a possible way of reducing population growth once a country has decided that the optimal population has been reached or will be in the near future.

2
THE ECONOMICS
OF ABORTION REPEAL

Very few of the major issues of our time are purely economic, and abortion is no exception. An economist is in no way qualified to answer the pivotal question of whether life begins at conception, at 24 weeks, or at birth. Nor can he summarily state whether or not laws to permit abortion should be passed. What he does have to offer is an analysis of those economic aspects of abortion which constitute an important part of the problem. Let's see how much light economics can throw on the issue.

The performance of an abortion, except in extraordinary circumstances, has long been a criminal activity in the United States. Therefore it is impossible to obtain accurate figures on the number of women who have undergone the operation, the percentage among them injured as a consequence of unsanitary abortion conditions, or the mortality rate. Nevertheless, some crude estimates point up the magnitude of the situation.

In New York before the legalization of abortion in 1970, it was estimated that a qualified doctor charged about $1,000 for the illegal operation. On Canada's west coast the price is approximately $500. More than 350,000 women are admitted annually to hospitals in the U.S. with complications resulting from abortions. Finally, it is estimated that more than 1,000 women die each year from improperly performed pregnancy terminations.

Even allowing for a very large percentage error in these estimates, it is clear that illegal abortion has been, and continues to be, big business, and that the number of women who undertake both the risk of criminal prosecution and the danger of crippling infection or death is substantial.

Laying aside for the moment any analysis of states where abortion has been legalized, let's begin by looking at the economics of illegal abortion, the situation now prevailing in most sections of the U.S. Who is willing to perform the illegal activity and at what price? A doctor convicted of performing an illegal abortion faces not only criminal prosecution but also expulsion from his profession, and the consequent lifetime loss of his M.D. license and livelihood. In addition he may have to endure ostracism by a community which regards him as a criminal. In short, the costs to a doctor of such a criminal conviction are immense. Yet, in many communities there are doctors whose strong moral convictions make them willing to bear these risks. Reputable doctors do perform abortions every day; and those who do not are sometimes willing to refer patients to other physicians who will take these risks (at a price). However many, perhaps most, pregnancy terminations are performed by unlicensed abortionists in unsanitary conditions. The referral has often been by word of mouth from, say, the local hairdresser. It is apparent that varying numbers of people, both qualified M.D.s and less qualified laymen, are willing to perform illegal abortions. The number and proficiency of those available differ according to the price women are willing to pay.

At the top of the scale—perhaps $800 to $1,000—is the licensed physician who is willing to perform the illegal activity at a price which compensates for the recognized risk. Below that are doctors for whom various admixtures of moral values and risk determine the price. A few with strong moral conviction will perform the operation for only $100–$200. But most abortionists asking a price that low are unlicensed, poorly qualified practitioners whose product can hardly be guaranteed. A rating scale would show relatively few licensed M.D.s willing to perform abortions at the $100–$200 level with the number growing as an increased price tends to compensate more adequately for the risk.

The illegality of abortions has, of course, increased the costs of both supplying and obtaining information, as we will show is also the case with euphorics. Information is never free, even in legalized activities, since it costs money to acquaint potential buyers with the location, quality, and price of a good or service. But in the case of an illegal activity the providing of information is even more expensive. The abortionist cannot advertise; and the more widely he lets his availability be known, the more likely he is to incur arrest. While some doctors unwilling to perform an abortion do refer patients to other, more lenient M.D.s, the referral is itself illegal and therefore risky. There are other ways of obtaining information about the professional competence of an abortionist, but how reliable is the local hairdresser? The high cost of information has its effects: Women seeking an abortionist are not able to inform themselves of all the possibilities without spending lots of time and money.

Contrast these conditions with those that exist where abortion is legal, quick, and safe. Information is no more costly to disseminate or to obtain than it is for other medical specialties such as pediatrics or dermatology. Specialists can be listed in the classified section of the telephone directory and with the county medical association. Anyone seeking a specialist can consult these sources or ask any physician for a referral.

Once the risks associated with illegality are removed, what governs the price at which a doctor is willing to perform a legal abortion? The M.D. who charges $800 for the illegal operation will no longer command that high price, since other doctors will now be willing to perform the operation for less. But how much less? We can get some idea if we see how a doctor values his time while working. Suppose he agrees to perform an appendectomy during a busy week. He may charge perhaps $100 for spending an extra half-hour doing it. If, instead, he chose to perform an abortion which would also require a half-hour, he would not be earning a fee for removing the infected appendix. His forgone earnings for the half-hour spent in performing the abortion instead of the appendectomy amount to $100. *Opportunity cost* has thus determined the value of the service, and he now has some idea of how much to charge for the abortion.[1] This basic determination does not, of course, include any special equipment or facilities. When legalizing abortions, some states have stipulated that they must be performed in a hospital. This requirement obviously substantially raises the price to be paid. To the doctors' opportunity costs must then be added the charges for hospital facilities utilized during the half-hour, which could perhaps mean $150 added to the cost of a pregnancy termination.

This simplified example by no means indicates that a single supply price could be expected to prevail among all doctors for performing legal abortions. The quality of a doctor's services varies according to his training, experience, and innate ability. But even given this consideration we should note that the overall relationship between the quantity of abortions supplied by M.D.s and the price they are paid to perform the operation is different after abortion repeal. It is still true that doctors will perform more abortions at higher fees because the increasing size of the reward induces them to forfeit doing other things. But at any particular fee, there will be more M.D.s willing to perform the operation when it is legal than when it is illegal, because the risks are removed. Note also that the quality of the service would in general be higher, since nonqualified practitioners would have little place in the picture if the operation were fully legalized.

[1] This assumes that competition among doctors would force the price to this level. For a qualification of this point as well as an examination of what determines doctors' opportunity costs, see Chapter 9, "The Economics of Medical Care."

Let us turn for a moment from the supply of legal abortions to the demand for illegal ones. The potential "buyer" of an illegal abortion faces a whole range of prices for the operation. Which will be chosen (i.e., what is the *demand schedule*)? Three simple examples show the process of decision.

The wife of a rich executive visits a travel agency which arranges a package tour to Japan. Included is round-trip air fare, an operation by a doctor in that country where abortions are legal, and three days subsequent sightseeing. The price tag: $2,000.

Next let's take a look at how the wife of a young lawyer earning $15,000 a year resolves her dilemma. She goes to her doctor; on the quiet he refers her to an M.D. willing to perform an illegal abortion for $500.

Then, there is the situation of the wife of a blue-collar worker making $5,000 a year. Surreptitiously asking around, she finds out from a worldly acquaintance that the local barber will do the operation in his back room for $200, aspirins included.

If we investigate the relative numbers of women in each of the above categories, we discover a definite pattern in which the costs and risks of acquiring information are important elements in each woman's decision. Only a few can afford and are willing to incur the expense of the Japanese tour; progressively more can and will pay the intermediate price; and many women seeking abortions feel that only the lowest price is within their reach.

It is easy to see how the costs of information can be prohibitively high for a woman at the lowest level of income. She is probably not the patient of a top-rank doctor who can refer her to a safe abortionist. If she arrives unreferred at the office of a highly placed O.B., he is unlikely to risk his neck by referring her to anyone he knows. Friends to whom she might turn are no better supplied with reliable information than she is.

It is not surprising that mortality from abortion appears to be inversely related to income. Better information is more available, with a correspondingly smaller risk, as the income level rises. We have seen that a woman's inability to uncover reliable information can lead her to choose dangerous alternatives in which she runs a high risk of crippling infection or even of death.

The statistics for New York City in the early 1960s support the plausibility of this argument: Private hospitals aborted one pregnant woman patient in 250; municipal hospitals, one in 10,100. The rate for whites was five times that for nonwhites and thirty times that for Puerto Ricans. Obviously, lower-income women were not having as many abortions performed by qualified M.D.s in hospitals as were upper-income women.

Under legal abortion, information costs are drastically reduced, since the prospective patient has only to ask her physician or consult the Yellow Pages. Moreover, when abortion carries the stigma of criminal activity, many women are unwilling to have the operation even if they do not want the child. By removing the stigma, legalization would result in a substantial increase in demand even at the same prices as before. But what would actually happen to prices in such an event?

It has already been shown that illegal abortion is offered at not one price, but many. The situation can be contrasted with the pricing of, say, an agricultural commodity such as wheat. At a moment in time, there is only one price quoted *for a particular kind and quality* of wheat. The essential information is known to all traders because all transactions are carried on in one central location: the Board of Trade in Chicago.[2] No such coordination exists in the case of illegal abortions. The quality of the product ranges from the skills of a highly experienced Japanese or American doctor to the haphazard methods of a back-alley quack. Such a wide range of qualifications can exist only because of the curtailment of the spreading of information among everyone involved. The result is, in effect, a whole series of separate

[2] Almost 90 percent of the noncommunist world's grain is bought and sold through one central location—the Chicago Board of Trade. These brokers have easy access to price and quality information for most parts of the globe.

situations arising from the unique conditions imposed by illegality. Even in the case of legal abortions there are variations in price and quality, although they are fewer and far less extreme. However, the "standard" price in the long run would clearly be much lower under conditions of legality.[3]

If, however, a state insists that abortions be performed only in a certified hospital, an illegal market will continue to exist. The additional hospital fees will keep the "standard" legal price well above that which low-income women can afford or are willing to pay. In such cases, back-room opportunists will very probably continue to provide illegal abortions at the "right" price. As long as a quack's opportunity cost plus his subjective evaluation of the risk involved is less than the price of a legal abortion, a market for the illegal service will exist.

As we have tried to show, economic analysis can give insight into the fundamental aspects of two opposite situations: in this case, illegal abortion vs. abortion reform or legalization. In the process, such analysis also undertakes to predict the effects of the transition. Abortion repeal will obviously benefit some people, but certainly not all, because no matter what course of action is taken, some gain and some lose. Economic analysis cannot, therefore, lead to an unquestioned policy recommendation.

[3] And even lower if there were free entry into the medical profession.

3
THE ECONOMICS
OF EUPHORIA

Marijuana is illegal; so are hashish, mescaline, dimethyl-triptamine, psilocybin, and tetrahydracannabinol. The illegality of these drugs does not, of course, prevent their use by young and old alike. It does, however, add certain peculiar characteristics to their production, distribution, and usage.

Before we look at drugs, we can learn a few things by examining an historical experience that proved unforgettable to most who lived through it—Prohibition.

On January 16, 1920, the 18th Amendment to the United States Constitution became effective. It prohibited ". . . manufacture, sale or transportation of intoxicating liquors within, or the import into, or export from the United States for beverage purposes." The Volstead Act, passed in 1919 to reinforce the 18th Amendment, forbade the purchase, possession, and use of intoxicating liquors.

A once-legal commodity became illegal overnight. The results were impressive, but certainly could have been predicted by any economist. Since the legal supply of liquor and wine fell to practically zero[1] while much of the public continued to demand the commodity, substitutes were quickly provided. Supplies of illegal liquor and wine flowed into the market. Increasing quantities of whiskey clandestinely found their way across the border from Canada, where its production was legal.

Of course, fewer entrepreneurs were now willing to provide the U.S. public with liquor. Why? Mainly because the cost of doing business suddenly increased. Any potential speakeasy operator had to take into account a high risk of being jailed and/or fined. He also faced increased costs in operating his bar, for the usual business matters had to be carried on in a surreptitious—i.e., more costly—way. Moreover, the speakeasy operator had to face the inevitable: an encounter with the Mafia. He could look forward to paying off organized crime in addition to the local cops. Payments to the former reduced the possibility of cement shoes and the East River. Payments to the latter reduced the probability of landing in jail.

As a general summation it could be said that Prohibition probably decreased the amount of alcoholic beverages that entrepreneurs were willing to provide *at the same prices as before*. If a bottle of one's favorite Scotch was available for $3 in 1919, either it would have cost more in 1920, or it would have been filled with a lower quality product.

Whiskey lovers faced another problem during Prohibition. They could no longer search the newspaper ads and billboards to find the best buys in bourbon. Information had gone underground, and even knowledge about quality and price had suddenly become a much dearer commodity. In general, consumers have several means of obtaining information. They can find out about products from friends, from advertisements, and from personal experience. When goods

[1] The exception was wine intended for religious purposes. The use of so-called "sacramental" wine increased by 800,000 gallons in the two years following ratification of the 18th Amendment, leading to interesting speculation about whether Prohibition somehow made Americans suddenly more religious.

are legal, they can be trademarked for identification. The trademark cannot be copied, and the courts protect it. Given such easily identified brands, consumers can be made aware of the quality and price of each via the recommendations of friends and ads. If their experience with a product does not jibe with their anticipations, they can assure themselves of no further encounter with the "bad" product by never buying that brand again.

When a general class of products becomes illegal, there are fewer ways of obtaining information on product quality. Brand names are no longer protected by the law, so falsification of well-known ones ensues. It becomes difficult to determine which trademarks are the "best." We therefore can understand why some unfortunate imbibers were blinded or killed by the effects of bad whiskey. The risk of something far more serious than a hangover became very real.

For some, the new whiskey-drinking costs were outweighed by the illicit joys of the speakeasy atmosphere. But other drinkers with more sensitive ethics were repelled by liquor's illegality and were deterred from consuming as much as they had before Prohibition, even if it had been obtainable at the same price as before.

While it is difficult to assess the net effect of these considerations, one fact is clear. The impact of Prohibition differed between rich and poor.

The high-income drinker was not particularly put out at having to pay more for whiskey of the kind he wanted. He ran little risk of being blinded, because neither the high price tag nor the cost of obtaining information about quality and supply could separate him from his favorite beverage. Presumably he would have been quite willing, before Prohibition, to pay more than the going price.

On the contrary, some lower-income imbibers had probably been paying just about their top limit for whiskey of acceptable quality before Prohibition. The sudden rise in costs left them two alternatives: Do without or settle for less, in the form of bootleg booze and bathtub gin. The

distribution of injury, sickness, and death due to drinking
contaminated whiskey directly mirrored the distribution of
income.

The analogy is obvious between what happened during
Prohibition and what is now happening with respect to most
euphorics and hallucinogens. Like bootleg liquor, these
drugs share the stricture of illegality which leads to both
relatively high costs and high risk in their manufacture, distribution, sale, and consumption. Yet there is a difference
between the two periods in the matter of who obtains the
more-wanted product. The wealthy user still is able to buy
quality; he may even pay intermediaries to do his shopping
around. But while the middle-income user ends up getting
inferior drugs, the "heads," or high-consumption users, who
are also poor, probably often get hold of the better-quality
euphorics, and often at prices below those paid by others.
The reason for this situation involves a mixture of economics
and sociology. First, these people would not be poor unless
they were working at low-paying jobs—if they are working
at all. Therefore, when they spend time away from their jobs
not much is lost, and we say that the opportunity cost of
their not working is low compared to those with higher-
paying jobs who must sacrifice more earnings when they
choose not to work. The poor user merely responds to his
low opportunity cost when he spends more time seeking
out the best buys in the drugs he urgently wants. This was
true during Prohibition, also, but it didn't have as much
import because there was not then such a large sociological
class of "heads" devoted to the whiskey "cult."

On the other hand, the problems that face a middle-
income drug user are manifold. If he spends time seeking
out information about which euphorics to buy and where
to find them, he is confronted with higher opportunity costs
for his time away from work. Potential jailing is a greater
deterrent in terms of both opportunity costs and psychic
and emotional costs. And since he is probably unable or
unwilling to pay some intermediary to do his searching for
him (as the rich user would do), he ends up with drugs of

a quality that would be scorned by many low-income "heads."

A parallel, and a question, might be found in the case of abortion operations. We noted in Chapter 2 that many rich women fly to Japan to have a legal abortion performed. Since the use of certain drugs is quite legal in other countries, why don't rich users fly overseas to obtain and use their drugs? Take the case of Nepal, where high-quality marijuana can be purchased for about 2 cents per ounce, while the price in the U.S. might run as high as $40 for the same quality and quantity. The relative price of the Nepalese euphoric is thus 1/2,000 that of the U.S. euphoric. Or is it? When we consider the *total* cost, we see that we must include round-trip air fare to Nepal, plus the opportunity cost of the flight time (minus any monetary value placed on seeing that exotic country). The relative price of 1 ounce of legal Nepalese marijuana now becomes more like $\left(\dfrac{\$.02 + \$800}{\$40} \right) = 20$ times the U.S. price for illegal marijuana.[2]

Up to now we've been dealing mainly with the demand side of the illegal drug picture. We have looked at the determinants of how much people buy and how much they are willing to pay for a certain quality of euphorics. Now let's look briefly at the supply side. We wish to find out what determines how much people are willing to furnish of a certain quality of euphoric at different prices. The parallels to be made with the supply of whiskey during Prohibition are numerous. The illegality of the manufacture and distribution of most drugs poses a large risk to suppliers. The risk is higher the greater (a) the probability of detection, (b) the probability of conviction, and (c) the potential jail sentence and/or fine. Costs of doing business include

[2] The added cost to the user of detection, conviction, and jail are, of course, not included in the $40 price for U.S. euphoric. However, the probability of detection and the costs of conviction are sufficiently low in the U.S. so as not to induce anyone to pay 20 times more for the pleasure of smoking marijuana in Nepal without fear of arrest.

measures to assure secrecy and avoid detection, payoffs to organized crime (for certain drugs not easily manufactured, like heroin), and potential payoffs to the police.

What would happen if marijuana were legalized? Should we expect a general state of euphoria?

On the supply side, entrepreneurs would be able to supply larger quantities at the same price as before because the costs of doing business would fall. There would be no risks involved, no requirement for payoffs to organized crime, and no high cost of maintaining secrecy in production and distribution. The price of many drugs would eventually fall to a level just covering the lower costs of legal production and legal distribution.

When there is unrestrained competition among the sellers of a legal product, it is difficult for relatively inferior products to exist side by side with better ones unless the price of the former is lower. Otherwise sellers of the superior product will inform the buying public of the anomaly. Since the product is legal, the free flow of information will assure that some buyers will refuse to purchase inferior products unless their price is correspondingly lower.

By opening the door to advertising, legalization would also reduce the costs of disseminating and obtaining information about supplies. Competition among sellers and increased information available to buyers would combine to raise the quality of the product.

On the demand side, legalization would, of course, reduce to zero the threats of detection, conviction, and jail, with their attendant costs. Because of higher overall quality, the risk of bad side effects from improperly prepared drugs would be lessened. Both of these cost reductions would lead consumers to demand a larger quantity even at the prices which had prevailed before legalization.

It is difficult to predict whether the price would rise or fall immediately after legalization. Since consumers presumably would demand more, suppliers would produce more. If the increase in demand were to exceed that in supply, a shortage would be the result and consumers would find themselves paying high prices to obtain as much of the now-legal product as they wanted. In the long run, however, it could safely be predicted that prices would, as usual, fall to a level just covering the costs of production, distribution, and normal profit—which would certainly be lower than the price paid today.

If drugs were to be legalized and this chain of events occurred, one more link in the sequence would be a fall in the price of euphorics relative to that of alcoholic beverages. Would this lead to a trend away from drinking—and towards the smoking of marijuana, for example? The answer hinges on an "if." If marijuana is a *substitute* for alcohol, this might well happen. But if the two are *complementary* instead of substitutable, then increased use of marijuana would lead to increased use of alcohol.

In any event, the above analysis does not constitute an argument for or against legalization of euphorics. There are costs to society involved in each course. There are also benefits. Describing the costs of making something illegal does not necessarily argue for a change in the law. After all, there are costs involved in passing a law which forbids wife abandonment, but society obviously has decided that the benefits of making abandonment illegal far outweigh them.

THE ECONOMICS
OF AUTOMOBILE SAFETY
STANDARDS

As the American public has become increasingly concerned
with safety on the highway, more and more Congressmen
have promoted legislation compelling car manufacturers to
install certain safety features on all new cars coming out of
Detroit. We now have twenty federal safety standards requiring such features, ranging from the most obvious—
padded dashboards and safety belts—to the most obscure
—nonactivating stop lamps on towed vehicles that become
separated. Without delving into the technical efficiency of
such requirements, we will attempt in this chapter to explain
the economic effects of safety legislation. In so doing we
should first briefly look at the way the automobile industry
operates and see what goes into the costs of making a Vega
or a Gremlin.

There are certain costs that the manufacturer must incur
no matter how many or how few of a new-model car he
sells. These costs include initially, those of design and marketing research to determine what will sell best. Once the
decision is made to produce a certain model, the costs of
tooling up must be considered—that is, making new body

dies, jigs, features, and new engine tools and molds. Then follow all the costs of setting up the production line for the new car. And, if the new model is to be accepted by the public, it has to be introduced via promotion—i.e., TV ads, billboards, and radio commercials—all of which involve costs.

All of the above are called *fixed* or *"sunk"* costs. Once they have been incurred by the auto manufacturer they are gone forever, whether the car is bought by 100 people or by 100,000.

In addition to these costs, there are others which vary according to the number of cars produced, the most obvious being for labor and material inputs. The more cars that are made, the more man-hours are required and the higher the manufacturer's total wage bill. And the more cars made, the more steel used, the more upholstery bought, the more steering wheels ordered, thus the higher the bill for total materials. Costs in this latter group are called *variable* because they fluctuate with output, although the relationship need not be one to one.

In addition to all this, we must realize that the car company has to make a profit or go out of business. In a competitive industry and in the long run, the rate of profit for one firm is usually not much higher than for any other, although differences obviously exist.

However, it seems difficult to classify the auto industry as competitive when one examines the profits of General Motors relative to Ford, Chrysler, and American Motors, or even relative to the average for all manufacturing firms. There have been numerous explanations for GM's rather remarkable capacity to make relatively high profits. One of these involves a phenomenon known as *economies of scale*, or more familiarly, *gains from mass production*. This means that when GM doubles *all* its inputs, its output more than doubles. Thus the larger its production, the smaller is its average cost per unit. By producing millions of cars, GM can charge the same price as other companies while clearing higher profits on each car sold. But we are left with a question: Why doesn't GM lower its prices below their present level (for it would still be making a profit) and eventually capture a larger and larger share of the market until no other company exists? We suspect that if GM really enjoys the reputed economies of scale, the reason it fails to act this way and drive all other makers out of business is the looming potential of an antitrust suit. GM does not want to be broken into bits as was Rockefeller's Standard Oil in 1911.

What, then, determines the price we pay for new cars? In the *short run* each company will make the most money if it ignores sunk costs (letting bygones be bygones). It should sell cars up to that number at which the revenue from selling an additional automobile will not cover the costs of producing it. The price which gives a company the biggest profits will be about equal to the costs involved in making that hypothetical final car.

We all know, of course, that no car maker is likely to figure things out by the slide rule of this analytic procedure.[1] We also know, however, that in the *long run* the manufacturer has to cover all costs and earn a "reasonable" profit or the owners will go into another business where they can make more money.

What, then, is the implication of this latter statement in the matter of required safety features? It is simply that the costs of such amenities will, sooner or later, be paid by the consumer. Seat belts, collapsible steering columns, and dual braking systems require additional resources. Somebody must pay for them, and eventually the tab will be picked up by the buyer of the car, although the manufacturer may share the costs if he is earning more than a competitive profit to start with.

Government regulation of safety features on cars has already raised the price of cars higher than it would have been otherwise.[2] Unless the quantity of cars that people demand is totally unresponsive to changes in the price, when the prices goes up, fewer cars will be bought. Some families

[1] We can predict behavior using this theory, though, even if the individual decision-makers do not reason this way.

[2] When *marginal costs* are increased, so, too, is price.

will have fewer cars, or will trade in their cars less often, or will depend more on taxis, buses, and trains.

Since imported cars are a substitute for American-made ones, U.S. companies have had every interest in prodding Congress to impose federal safety standards uniformly on *all* cars. Otherwise the relative price of imported automobiles would have fallen and more people would have bought them than before, at the expense, of course, of domestic car sales.

Whether more lives will be saved with the existence of, and compliance with, federal automobile safety standards is an empirical question. Regardless of the answer, the improvements are not free; increased safety requires the use of real resources, and thus raises a fundamental issue which cannot be resolved here, but which we should think about. Suppose the new safety standard saves 100, or even 1,000, lives a year at an additional price of, say, $50 million in costs to the consumer. Is it worth it? At some price we can make every car a tank and completely safe for its occupants. Since very few people would care to pay the price of a tank, such an expedient might also solve some problems of pollution and congestion, but it is doubtful that the idea would meet with overwhelming enthusiasm from consumers. In fact, if they were offered a tradeoff of various increasing degrees of safety in their cars but at successively higher prices, we would probably find that a great many people would not opt for higher levels of safety. Most would be willing to accept additional risk in trade for a lower-priced automobile.

It is perfectly clear that we do indeed place a price value on life, even though such an idea seems objectionable. At some price we can obviously eliminate automobile accidents, but we do not choose this solution. Where, then, do we draw the line?

Each individual makes some decision on the value of his own life when he decides whether to take a train or drive a car, whether to work in a dangerous occupation (at relatively high pay) or to work in a safe one (at lower pay). Most people *say* that a human life (especially their own) is "price-less." Human behavior today does not support this state-ment. Do you spend all of your resources in preventing any possibility of accident?

Of course, there still exists an argument for imposing safety standards, even if drivers must pay more for their cars. Certain drivers' actions can affect others who have no say in the matter. If a driver has poor brakes, he may run over pedestrians who may never be fully compensated for their injuries. Thus safe brakes are required on all cars. Note, however, that this argument does not apply to padded dashes, for example, which protect only the car's occupants.

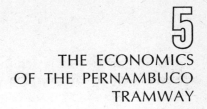

THE ECONOMICS
OF THE PERNAMBUCO
TRAMWAY

It sounds plausible. The price of gas, water, oil, electricity, housing, transport—you name it—is too high! So, set a lower price and provide a system of enforcement that prevents chiselers from getting away with illegal prices. Does it work? We might label one attempt the Pernambuco Tramway syndrome, and pass it off as a fairy tale.

Once upon a time, there was a foreign company that received a franchise to build a streetcar system in the growing city of Pernambuco, Brazil. They built the system and people rode back and forth on the streetcars. The original fare (Who can remember way back then?) was one-tenth of a cruzeiro.

It is important to note that the rate was fixed by government edict, and that the foreign company received a return on its investment equal to what it could have obtained with other uses of its funds, or maybe a little higher. (That is, it equaled or exceeded the opportunity costs of the firm's capital.) Now as time went by, the real value of the cruzeiro began to fall because inflation set in. As the beleaguered cruzeiro dropped from one cent to half a cent to a quarter of a cent, the fare—still fixed by edict—no longer produced enough revenue to cover the costs of the system. After a while it could not even cover the costs of current operations (variable costs). The company actually lost money every time a streetcar ran down the street. The company tightened its billfold. It certainly was not going to put more money into the system; so the cars and rails deteriorated. Every once in a while a loose rail came up through the floorboards and spitted a passenger like a roast pig. Actually, by this policy of reducing the quality of service, the tramway operators were raising the real price to users, who now were paying the same fare for a service of pretty dubious value. The streetcars stood empty most of the time. When last heard from, the company was trying to curtail schedules and to sell, or even to give, the operation to the government. This is one fairy tale without a happy ending. But why worry about it?

In New York City since World War II people have lived under a system of rent controls. And because that situation is no fairy tale, perhaps we should examine its consequences a little more closely.

To do so, we have to examine what happens in the short run, when the amount of rental housing is fixed, as opposed to the long run when the supply of housing can be varied. Before rent control, prices were determined by competition among renters and among landlords. Any particular price had to be mutually agreeable to both parties or no lease would be signed. When controls were imposed, a ceiling was set on many apartment rental fees. Obviously, if this ceiling exceeded the existing rent, nothing happened. But, as time went on and inflation took its toll, the prices of everything, including apartments, started to rise. At some point, imposed rent ceilings inevitably fell below the level that landlords and prospective tenants could have agreed upon in the absence of any restrictions.

Anyone who has apartment-hunted in New York knows the quite predictable result. It is literally impossible to find an apartment anywhere near the main part of the city, because numbers of people are eager to get a lease on an apartment at rent-controlled prices. A gap has been artificially established between available supplies and actual demand. An economist would say that the rent-controlled rate has been set below *equilibrium*.

Since more housing is demanded than is available at the controlled price, the supplier can set his own terms for the lineup of prospective renters. He can accept bribes in the form of "key money" or other subterfuges; or he can discriminate among prospective renters on the basis of race, color, religion, kids, dogs, or what have you. Even so, it is a rare case when he can actually make as much money as would have been feasible without rent control.

The fortunate renter who finally signs a lease is now in the driver's seat. Having leased at rent-controlled rates, he can, if he chooses, sublease his apartment at a much higher going rate. He then benefits where the landlord could not. This may appear to some a "correct" form of income redistribution, but rent control has pernicious long-run side effects. Whatever its condition, the landlord can rent an apartment continually at the controlled price. More importantly, who bothers to invest in more housing? Obviously, most entrepreneurs consider it a losing proposition, or there would not be such a critical housing shortage in New York City today. If an investor can get 9 percent for his money in some investments, then this is the opportunity cost of his capital, and he will not tie it up in housing where rent controls restrict the return to 6 percent. The result is a perennial shortage, and a continuing necessity for the landlord to distribute (ration) the available rental space on whatever discriminatory grounds he chooses.

What many people want is more housing, so that the supply offered at all prices will increase sufficiently to lower the *equilibrium price* and make housing cheaper (shift the supply schedule outward to the right). Yet rate-fixing of the type described operates in exactly the opposite direction. We can get the desired result only when the return on capital invested in housing exceeds the opportunity cost of capital invested in other activities. Investors will then be glad to supply the market with more housing, the price will fall, and we will have cheaper housing.

It would be reassuring to discover that the rent-control situation is unique, but it has many companions. We face a natural-gas crisis, a garbage-disposal crisis, a water-shortage crisis, and an electricity crisis. While some of these crises also involve other problems, a major factor in each is a price set so low that the amount demanded at that price exceeds the amount suppliers are willing to offer, resulting in a shortage.

In the case of electric power, the consequences are becoming more and more widespread, as indicated by brownouts, blackouts, and sometimes rationing. As in some other industries, such as transportation and water systems, the supplier of electricity faces a problem which a single rate exacerbates. The demand for his product at the fixed rate is not constant, but is subject to peak periods. In the case of electricity, the brownouts occur at these periods of extraordinary demand. On the eastern seaboard, for example, the peak demand comes during the hot days of summer when electric air conditioners are whirring. In the Northwest, by contrast, the demand peaks as a result of electric space heating in cold weather. Variations in demand are not only seasonal, but occur within a day. In some areas the heaviest use comes from 5:00 p.m. to 10:00 p.m., followed by a relatively light demand until 7:00 a.m. In short, we have an industry which has unused capacity for much of the year, and for a good part of every day, but which is strained beyond its capacity for short intervals. To be able to meet these peak demands, the typical electric utility may have to maintain so much excess equipment that it will be operating, on the average, at only 55 percent of capacity.

It is not hard to pinpoint the economics behind the problem. Under a single, uniform rate for electricity, the peak-load user is being subsidized by all other consumers, since the costs of maintaining excess equipment are shouldered equally by all users. If the power company were to adjust the single rate, charging higher prices for peak-period use than for other times, available evidence indicates that less would be demanded at the more costly periods. Peak-period use would tend to level off, while the lower price during slack periods would encourage greater use at those times. Skillful planning along such lines might effectively eliminate overloads and their resultant brownouts and blackouts.

Is such an adjustment of the single rate practical? Would it work? It does in France today. Beginning in 1954, *Electricité de France* instituted a multitariff pricing system for electricity, the different rates being set to best approximate the actual cost of supplying the additional electricity for any specific season and time of day. For example, because in the summer months, demand is greatest during the day, a higher price is set for the daylight hours than for the night. The differential pricing also takes into account changes in sources of supply. Because winter cuts off the flow of water for hydroelectric stations, more expensive thermal generation must be used. Therefore, French consumers pay more for electricity in winter than in summer. After a careful examination of the French experience, one economist wrote that "clear improvement over the [old] pricing scheme is very plausibly claimed."[1]

With minor modifications, peak-load pricing can also solve or ameliorate problems related to water shortages and to transport congestion, as well as those of other industries with similar demand and cost patterns.

[1] Thomas Marschak, "Capital Budgeting and Pricing in the French Nationalized Industries," *Journal of Business* (January 1960), p. 151.

6

THE ECONOMICS
OF PROSTITUTION

In 1945, a French politician—one Mme. Marthe Richards—
demanded closure of all Paris brothels. She claimed that the
178 licensed houses, 600 prostitute-serving hotels, 10,000
pimps, and 6,600 ladies of the night were "undermining
Parisian morals and health." Moreover, she estimated that
the closing of brothels would make available 6,000 rooms
for students and those bombed out of their homes during
the war.

The Municipal Council of Paris, impressed by her statistics,
gave the brothels three months to shut down. The effects
have been far-reaching, to say the least, and apparently have
not proved too satisfactory, because recently a vigorous
campaign has been shaping up in France to restore the legality of the world's oldest profession. Although the product
differs considerably, the economic analysis of prostitution
is similar to those of abortion and euphoria, with, of course,
a few new twists.

The service that prostitutes offer for sale has, like all
others, two dimensions: quantity and quality. In some sense,
these two are interrelated; quantity can be increased by

lowering quality. The quality of the service is, among other things, a function of (a) experience (*human-capital investment*);[1] (b) the innate characteristics of the provider of the services, such as looks and intelligence; and (c) current operating expenditures such as how much money is spent on appearance, surroundings, and health.

To be sure, *substitution* is possible among these three aspects of quality. Perhaps the same quality can be achieved either by being born beautiful or by spending effort and money on make-up and clothes. Some ladies of the night are able to compensate for poor looks by dressing well. We say that they are able to substitute clothes for natural endowments.

For many who utilize the services of a prostitute, the health aspect of quality is of utmost importance. The decision to make prostitution illegal in France has notable consequences on the probability of some clients contracting venereal disease. Let's see why.

When prostitution was legal, numerous business establishments existed whose purpose in life was offering prostitutes' services. Since all was on the up and up, they could advertise without risk. Because clients could easily compare prices and qualities, information was relatively cheap. If it became common knowledge that the employees of one house spread venereal disease to their customers, that firm would either have to lower its prices drastically or suffer a drop in clientele.

Even though cheap information made it inadvisable for any firm to allow unhealthy employees to work (because clients would go elsewhere), the French government made doubly sure that venereal disease was kept at a minimum by requiring weekly medical inspections. Since most prostitutes worked in establishments, it was relatively easy to check all of them, and social disease was rare among prostitutes before 1947. The reader can easily draw the analogy between legalized prostitution and legalized abortions and narcotic usage.

[1] You are making an investment in your own human capital by attending college and by reading this book.

When prostitution was legal, suppliers of the service charged their opportunity cost, with no "risk" factor added, since no threat of imprisonment or fines existed. Those demanding the service had no need to invest large amounts of their resources (time and effort) obtaining information that would help them avoid the risk of a poor-quality product, as represented by the threat of venereal disease.

What has happened in France since 1947? Obviously there are no more legal houses of prostitution. The girls, for the most part, have taken to the streets. The cost of doing business has increased. Streetwalkers must avoid detection and arrest either by cleverness or by paying off police. Some girls must stay outside more than before, adding a cost of discomfort. Also, they no longer benefit from economies of scale that previously kept down the cost of such "accessories" to their trade as an attractive atmosphere.

At the same wages as before, fewer prostitutes were willing to stay in the profession after 1947.[2] On the demand side, clients could no longer be so confident about the quality of the product, because competition among legal houses was removed. Previously, any house that got a bad reputation suffered. But now individual prostitutes can more easily lower quality (i.e., have V.D.) and still obtain clients, for information has become much more difficult to obtain. And, of course, there are no longer government medical inspections. (Such a situation would be tantamount to a system of FDA inspection and labeling of different grades of marijuana in our own country.)

Predictably, as information about quality has become more expensive, the wealthy citizen has been the one able to pay the cost of seeking out the healthy prostitutes, while the poor have contracted veneral disease. If a poor woman suffers from a bad abortion, the rest of society bears little of the cost. If a middle-class marijuana user dies from some arsenic in his illegal cigarette, the rest of society bears little of the cost. But if a dock worker contracts V.D., he is not alone in bearing the cost. Other parts of society must also

---

[2] The *supply schedule* shifted inward to the left.

pay, because he can spread the disease to others. This problem explains in part why there is right now so much fervor in France about legalizing prostitution again: The rates of V.D. have soared among those associated with the prostitution industry (suppliers and demanders alike).

In summary, the prohibiting of prostitution in France caused a decrease in the number[3] and in the average quality of prostitutes, probably a decrease in the number of demanders (even at the same prices as before), and probably a rise in the average price to the customer. As an added effect, V.D. became more common among common folk.

[3] Or in the rate of growth.

7
THE ECONOMICS
OF RAISING LESS CORN
AND MORE HELL

When Mary Lease stumped the Kansas countryside in 1890, she urged the farmers to raise "less corn and more hell," and that's just what they have been doing ever since.

In the late nineteenth century, their activities took the form of political campaigns aimed in several directions: (a) to expand the money supply, which they felt would increase agricultural prices faster than other prices; (b) to introduce railroad rate regulation designed to lower freight rates for transporting agricultural products; and (c) to curb monopolies, which they felt would reduce their costs for commodities. When prices of farm goods rose at the start of the twentieth century, the farmers stuck to raising their corn, and during World War I they expanded their production dramatically in response to soaring prices. Then, after the war, European countries imposed high taxes on any agricultural goods crossing their borders. Along with other factors, this restriction reduced the amount of corn that American farmers could sell. Farm prices fell sharply, and farm organizations in the 1920s began to view their problem as one of relative overproduction. Numerous cooperative efforts were made to restrict production; but these efforts failed (except in a few specialty crops such as tobacco, where the relatively small number of producers made mutual agreement more feasible). Most crops were produced under competitive conditions: A large number of sellers (and buyers) dealt in a product which was undifferentiated (one farmer's corn was just the same as another farmer's corn). Accordingly, it was impossible for producers to organize themselves on a voluntary basis. But what farmers failed to do by voluntary cooperation in the 1920s, they accomplished via governmental directives in the 1930s. The result was the farm price-support program which, with many modifications and changes, is still with us today.

We can see the results best by first examining the market for agricultural commodities prior to price supports. In that competitive market, a large number of farmers supplied a commodity—in our example, corn. The sum of the quantities that individual farmers will supply at various prices makes up the *aggregate supply schedule* of a commodity. Each farmer supplies only a small part of the total quantity of corn. He cannot influence the price of this product. If he raised his price anyone wishing to purchase corn could easily buy from someone else at the going (equilibrium) price. And no farmer would sell below the going price because he would make less money than possible, since he could sell all that he produced at the going price. Thus, every unit of output farmers sell goes for the same price. The price received for the last (*marginal*) unit sold is exactly the same as that received for all the rest.

The farmer will produce corn up to the point at which, if he produced one more unit, its production costs would be greater than the price received. Every farmer faces the same production decision. Notice that at higher prices, farmers can incur higher costs for additional units produced and still make a profit; so at higher prices all farmers together will produce more. But again, no farmer alone can influence the price. No farmer will stop producing until he stops making a profit. That is, each farmer will end up selling corn at the going price, which will equal his costs of production plus a *normal profit*.[1]

The price at which each farmer can sell his corn depends on how people feel about buying it, and that depends on their tastes, incomes, and the prices of substitute staples such as wheat. The demand for food in general is quite unresponsive to price changes because there are no close substitutes. The demand for corn is somewhat more responsive to price changes because of available substitutes. Even so, it takes a drastic reduction in the price of corn to get people to buy a lot more. Conversely, an increase in unit price causes people to buy much less. (The demand for corn is relatively *price inelastic*.) This situation has implications for farmers.

Agricultural costs of production and output can vary greatly from year to year because of, among other things, variations in weather. During a good year, production may be relatively large. But since the demand for corn is relatively inelastic, farmers will have to drastically reduce the price of their corn if they are to sell it all. They may even have to sustain a loss that year. The opposite situation occurs when production is small one year because of, say, a drought.

In sum, the short-run competitive market in corn resulted in changing prices of the product, changing profits for the producers.

Now how did the usual price-support program work? The government decided what constituted a "fair price." The formula for this vital determination was the ratio between the prices farmers historically paid for what they bought compared to the prices they received for their crops in "good" years. How can the government make this arbitrary price "stick" if it is above the level that would prevail otherwise?[2] It agrees to buy the corn at that (parity) price.[3] Actually the purchase is disguised as a loan from the Commodity

---

[1] This is actually a cost to society since it is required to keep him farming corn instead of changing to an alternative occupation.
[2] Called the market equilibrium price.
[3] This is one possibility only; there are others.

Credit Corporation that never need be repaid. The government then stores the corn. In return, the farmer must promise to restrict the acreage he plants by keeping part of his land uncultivated in a "soil bank."

The hope and expectation of the architects of the plan was that the restriction of acreage would cause production to fall so that, at the support price, the quantity demanded would be about the same as the amount supplied. Then the government wouldn't be forced to buy corn and store it. But the results have not fulfilled all expectations. Being human, the farmers tended to put their worst acreage in the soil bank and their most productive acreage into corn, whose sale at parity was now assured. Moreover, with less land to cultivate the farmer intensified his use of fertilizer, better seed, and technological know-how. Progress in the latter area has caused productivity to rise at a faster rate in agriculture than in industry.

The net result in many cases was a greater output from less acreage, and as of 1965 the government had purchased "surplus" crops worth more than $5.5 billion.

As an example of how responsive farmers can be to rising prices, let us consider the soybean case. During the Johnson administration, the support price of soybeans was raised from $2.25 per bushel to $2.50. By 1968 the government had been forced to buy 300 million bushels of surplus soybeans at $2.50 a bushel.

The response to falling prices has been just as emphatic. Consider what happened when, in 1969, Agricultural Secretary Hardin lowered the soybean price support from $2.50 back down to $2.25 per bushel. Instead of increasing output by 127 million bushels, as they had during the previous year when support prices were at the higher level, soybean growers increased production by a mere 13 million bushels.

Price supports mean two things, then: (a) higher prices to the consumer for those products whose fixed (parity) price exceeds the price that would otherwise prevail; and (b) more governmental resources (taxpayers' money) expended in agriculture than would be otherwise.

If it is true that price supports and acreage restrictions

actually increase the wealth of farmers, there should then be every incentive for more entrepreneurs to start new farms and to share in the profits. This incipient threat of new competition was met in an increasing way by the tobacco farmers. More than three decades ago, they found a way around the problem by fostering legislation which allotted to 500,000 growers the right to raise tobacco on lands then in use. For all practical purposes no new land has been put into production since then, because a prohibitive tax of 75 percent is levied on all tobacco grown on unlicensed land.

Owners of licensed land have thus been granted a monopoly in tobacco-growing. If you were to buy some of this land today, would you expect to make money as a monopolist? If you answered "Yes," you are in for a surprise. The price of land was long ago bid up to levels that yield new owners only a competitive rate of return. The ones who made money were the original holders of the tobacco licenses, who reaped profits to the tune of $1,500 to $3,000 per acre.[4]

Since the program for controlling tobacco production also includes restriction on how much leaf each owner can put up for sale and at what price he can sell it, the net results have been: (a) a smaller supply of tobacco than would otherwise have been provided, (b) a higher price for tobacco than would have prevailed under free competition, (c) a consequent higher price for tobacco products.

The implications of the last statement depend on the elasticity of demand for these products. If people smoke more or less the same quantity of cigarettes and cigars regardless of relatively small variations in price (i.e., if tobacco products face inelastic demand) then higher prices simply mean that more income will be devoted to tobacco products and less to other things. Since this seems to be the case, the tobacco program has thus resulted in a transfer of income from cigarette smokers to the original owners of the tobacco-growing licenses.

[4] F. H. Maier, J. L. Hedrick, and W. L. Bigson, Jr., *The Sale Value of Flue-Cured Tobacco Allotments*, Agricultural Experiment Station, V.P.I., Technical Bulletin No. 148 (April 1960).

In summary, all agricultural programs that involve price supports, acreage allotments, and crop control result in the consumers paying a higher price for the products. Whether one judges this result to be "good" or "bad" depends on his viewpoint as to whether farmers are the proper recipients of the gain, and whether consumers should pay for those gains. Ultimately, the decision boils down to whether it would be possible to leave everyone better off by using other, more economically efficient means.

8

THE ECONOMICS
OF USURY LAWS

Money-lenders have long been the targets for endless vituperative attacks as bloodsucking leeches on society. The stigma has been so great that dominant ethnic groups have historically shunned the occupation, leaving it to minorities to serve the borrowing needs of any given community, and consequently to endure victimization, purges, and bloodlettings when scapegoats were needed.

The Western world has certainly been no exception. The laws of the Church against usury were explicit, and it was left to the Jews to dominate the profession for many centuries. As happened with the Chinese in Malaysia and the Hindus in Africa in more recent times, they became a ready target for persecution.

The concept of *interest* for money lent dates back to Roman times when, by law, the defaulting party to a contract had to pay his creditor a compensation. Medieval lawyers used the legal tactic of *damna et interesse* to extract such compensation. Thus *interesse* became a charge for the use of money (under the guise of indemnity for failure to perform a contract).

It would be convenient to think that the opposition to money-lending for *interesse* resulted from an ancient ignorance of economic principles. After all, why should someone be willing to give up the use of his own money unless he were paid? Man's modern enlightenment on this topic has not, however, completely changed the picture. In fact, the persistence of legislation affecting the lending of money makes it clear that a widespread suspicion still lingers that the money-lender possesses some unique, shady, and monopolistic influence. Many states have enacted laws setting maximum rates of interest on loans to consumers, and the federal government has legislated the maximum interest rates for various uses of money. What are the consequences? To find out, we must examine the so-called "money market."

The market for money is like any other market. The suppliers are individuals and institutions who are willing at a price (the interest rate) to forgo present command over current use of goods and services; and the higher the price, the more money they will lend. The demanders are many: consumers wanting to buy goods now and pay later, investors undertaking some enterprise, and governments. And, as with other goods and services, the lower the price, the more will be demanded. So far, so good! But the money market in fact is composed of a lot of submarkets—those for consumer loans, commercial credit, and real estate, to name a few. Each submarket has its own institutions—consumer loan companies, finance companies, banks, savings and loan associations—which specialize in bringing particular classes of borrowers and lenders together. Moreover, the price of money is different in each market. For financing the purchase of an automobile, the effective interest rate may be 18 to 24 percent per year; yet a corporation may be able to borrow for 7 percent, and the federal government for 5 percent. These rates also fluctuate over time with overall changes in the supply and demand for loans.[1]

[1] In addition, during periods of inflation these rates will go higher, reflecting the fact that suppliers are willing to loan money only at greater interest than before because when they are paid back the money will be worth less than it was when it was borrowed.

What concerns us, however, is an explanation of the variations in rates at any given moment in time. Several factors determine the differences, other things being equal. First is the length of the loan. The longer the time period involved, the less certain the lender can be about conditions at the time of repayment; consequently, he demands higher compensation. Second is the degree of risk. A lender who feels that a given loan is excessively risky will ask a high rate of interest. Finally, the cost of administering the loan must be considered. It frequently costs as much to handle a small loan as a large one; therefore, the "load" factor, or handling charge, is necessarily a much higher percentage of a small than a large loan. Since this is a charge added to the "pure" price, it implicitly shows up as a higher interest rate.

Each type of loan has its own characteristics. For example, automobile loans are more risky than most and impose a high handling cost. Corporate loans may be for a long or short period, and are subject to risk varying with the credit reputation of the company. Since they usually involve substantial amounts of money, the handling charges constitute a relatively small percentage of the total cost of such loans. The federal government issues short-term notes which are in effect riskless; because of the government's taxing power, they cannot be defaulted. They also involve substantial sums and therefore small handling charges per dollar involved. The net result of these factors is a relatively low rate of interest.

The suppliers of loanable funds can reasonably be expected to shift their funds from one submarket to another depending on where they can obtain the highest rate of return, adjusted for time, risk, and handling charges. However, they must have access to information on all of these possible outlets for their money. Since a wide variety of agencies and news media dispenses this information at very low cost, the overall capital market tends to be very responsive to changes which affect the rates of return to various suppliers.

To return now to the question of usury laws: Suppose a state legislates a maximum interest rate of 12 percent on consumer loans. If this is higher than the generally prevailing interest rate, it has no effect. However, this is an unlikely assumption. Even in the absence of inflationary tendencies, the going rate on run-of-the-mill consumer transactions is normally higher than 12 percent. What, then, is the effect of the restriction? At the lower rate, buyers will demand more money than the finance companies are willing to supply at that return. Lenders will begin by introducing service charges to cover "handling costs" which formerly were incorporated in the interest rate. Then they will move to some sort of rationing of the funds available for loans. Logically, they will attempt to eliminate the riskier loans; and since empirically the risk of default on loans is inversely related to the income of the borrower, the refusal of loans to the lowest-income groups will offer the easiest course—i.e., the least costly procedure in terms of acquiring information about potential borrowers. The predictable outcome, therefore, is that loans will be made only to the higher-income groups and the would-be borrower whose income is low will face a closed door.

Before turning from state usury laws to federal analogies, we should investigate the allegations of those who support a ceiling on interest rates. The charges cover two areas: (a) that a monopolistic conspiracy exists among loan companies to maintain a high rate of interest; and (b) that the interest rate is too high because of legislation, presumably inspired by the loan companies, to restrict entry of new companies into the consumer-finance field.

No *a priori* judgment is possible on either contention without an examination of conditions in the consumer-loan market in each state. In any case, however, the solution to the problem of rates that are higher than the competitive level cannot be found in the fixing of an arbitrary ceiling, for the reason just described. Rather, the solution must lie in vigorous prosecution of any conspiracy or in the repeal of laws unduly restricting entry into the field.

No usury laws exist at the federal level, but there are federal restrictions on the interest that commercial banks are allowed to pay for deposits. Just as restrictions on the interest rates for loans have been shown to exert certain economic effects, so, too, do restrictions on the interest payable by banks on deposits.

Commercial banks are forbidden to pay interest on the demand deposits (checking accounts) that they hold. What is the effect of this restriction? It must be understood that banks benefit from holding your money in a checking account. The amount you leave on deposit can be used for investment either in loans to other customers or in stocks, bonds, and real estate, all of which yield income to the bank. Banks, therefore, would quite willingly compete for your profitable dollars.

A zero interest payment restriction simply leads banks to compete in some other way.[2] You are offered "free" checking if your balance is kept above $200, "free" overdraft provisions if your balance exceeds $500, and personalized printed checks with pleasant pictures of sailing clippers embossed on them, at no extra charge. You are, therefore, receiving a valuable consideration (interest) on your checking account because you are charged less than cost for certain services.

Restrictions also govern how much interest can be paid for time deposits (savings accounts). When competition for funds would normally induce banks to offer higher interest rates, they must instead resort to giving away "free" hairdryers, clocks, and pens to new customers. During our most recent inflationary episode, as interest rates climbed steadily for corporate bonds of impeccable quality, the banks were hard pressed to compete for funds. Regulations were even invoked to prevent free giveaways from gaining too much value. As a result, savings and loan associations suffered large outflows of funds during the later 1960s and the start of the 1970s. After all, if a rate of return of 9½ percent is available on safe, Aaa-rated bonds, who would leave much money in a local savings account at 5 percent?

[2] The legal restriction actually grants all banks, taken together, a government enforced *monopsony* in the market for an input called "demand deposits." All the gimmicks mentioned below are merely each individual banks' method of "cheating" on the monopsonistic cartel.

The regulation of savings-account interest rates has had serious consequences in another sector of the economy, the housing market. Since funds were flowing out of savings and loan associations, the source of available mortgage money dried up, for this is where such companies do their investing. The dearth of funds, aided by other factors, led to a sharp drop in new housing starts by the latter part of the 1960s. In 1965, 1.4 million new units had been started, but only 1.1 million starts were made in 1966. Not until 1968 was the 1.4 million mark reached again, and at the time of this writing, the figure is still the same. By a circuitous but evident route, the regulation of savings accounts thus led to a "housing shortage" and to consequent higher housing prices.

Restrictions on economic variables always have consequences by which some gain and some lose. Economic analysis can help identify both the effects of the restrictions and the groups affected. Restrictions on interest rates lead to curtailment of the supply of loans, with lower-income groups being most adversely affected.

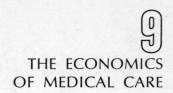

THE ECONOMICS
OF MEDICAL CARE

FACTS

1. Doctors earn more on the average than any other professional group.

2. The price of health-care services has risen much faster than other prices.

3. Doctors charge different prices for the same service to different people.

4. The American Medical Association has opposed some kinds of voluntary cooperative medical plans.

5. Medicare has turned out to cost much more than was anticipated.

6. Some people say that we should have free medical care, as in Britain.

REASONS

1. Doctors are relatively highly paid because the supply of doctors has not grown as fast as the demand.

2. The price of medical services has risen rapidly not only because of rising costs of inputs (doctors, nurses, equipment,

etc.), but also because of changes in the quality of medical care.

3. Doctors can discriminate in pricing because of the structure of the market.

4. The AMA has viewed some types of prepaid cooperative medical practice as a threat to the profession.

5. Medicare has cost much more than anticipated because the demand for medical care turned out to be more responsive to low prices than was previously imagined. Also, many doctors who had been treating elderly, indigent patients without charge could now be paid for providing such care.

6. There is no such thing as free medical care.

These six answers are accurate, if not very complete, explanations of some of the issues involved in the economics of medical care. An understanding of the factors underlying the first five explanations is essential to an intelligent assessment of the alternative program for medical care implied by the sixth statement. Let us go into more detail on each point.

1. The American Medical Association, when founded in 1847, adopted two basic policy positions: that doctors should be licensed, and that schools of medicine must be accredited. The first policy was quickly adopted by state legislatures, but the second was not enacted until state medical schools recommended that a substantial number of schools be closed and standards for the remainder be raised. State legislatures delegated the task of accrediting medical schools to the AMA. Since one could not receive a license to practice without graduating from an accredited school, the result was the restriction of the supply of licensed doctors to graduates of these schools. Severe accrediting requirements led to a reduction in the number of medical schools from 162 in 1904 to 69 in 1920. The 1904 figure was not reached again until the mid-1950s. As a consequence, the number of doctors per 100,000 people dropped from 157 in 1900 to 132 in 1957.

During this period the demand for doctors was growing as population and income increased. Since the demand for doctors is *income elastic*—that is, as people's incomes grow, they spend an increased portion of their additional income on medical care (including doctors)—there can be no doubt that the population as a whole desired to purchase an ever-increasing amount of doctors' services. But since there was no comparable increase in the number of medical students obtaining M.D. degrees, the supply of doctors did not keep pace with the rising demand. Accordingly, the price could be expected to rise, and it did. For the period 1939 to 1951, the mean income of physicians increased 218 percent, a substantially greater jump than occurred in any other profession.

2. Expenditures for medical care in the United States increased from under $4 billion in 1929 to approximately $40 billion in 1965. The first figure was about 4 percent of total national spending, while the second represents about 6 percent.[1] During the same period the prices of medical services rose at an annual rate of 2.5 percent; since 1947, they have risen at a rate of 3.5 percent, which is substantially higher than the annual percentage increase of an average of all other prices in the economy. The large increase in physicians' income accounts for a portion of this rise, but certainly only a fractional part, because doctors' fees are not all that is involved in the cost of medical care. Patients must also pay for hospital facilities and other equipment, as well as drugs, and the prices of these have also been rising at a rapid rate.

In addition, the quality of medical care has improved greatly. Therefore, some percentage of these increased prices is merely payment for a better product. This is a complex and controversial issue because it is extremely difficult to measure the quality of, for example, a physician's talents. Despite the difficulties, attempts have been made to assess quality levels, and they do suggest that some of the increase in price results from our getting more for our money.

3. When doctors charge different prices for essentially

---

[1] Remember, the demand for medical care is income elastic.

the same service to different patients, we say that they are *price discriminating*. To understand why a doctor would wish to set discriminatory fees, we need to look at a situation where competition does not exist. In such a case, the seller of a good or service is called a *monopolist*. If a monopolist can effectively group the buyers of his product according to how much they are willing to pay for it, he will then make more money, and he is labeled a discriminating monopolist. He obtains a higher income by charging each separate group "what the traffic will bear," rather than charging all people the same price. If he took the latter course, he would discourage some patients who were very responsive to price changes from buying his services. At the same time, he would not be extracting all the money possible from patients who were very unresponsive to price changes. However, he must be able to prevent those who are willing to pay only a relatively low price (have elastic demand) from buying at that price and reselling to those willing to pay a higher price (those with inelastic demand). Obviously doctors can effect this distinction because few medical services are transferable among patients. We usually find that doctors charge higher prices to patients with higher incomes. Apparently the amount that people are willing to pay for medical care is directly related to income.[2]

On closer examination of the individual doctor's situation, it is not so obvious that he can really act as a *discriminating monopolist* unless he is the only M.D. in a very isolated community. In most cases he is in competition with all other doctors around him. He then has an incentive to lower his prices to higher-income patients, knowing that by attracting more of them he can increase his total income. (He, of course, will not lower the rates below those charged low-income patients.) Since each competing doctor has this incentive, we should not observe price discrimination. The evidence suggests, however, that doctors *do* discriminate: The more opulent members of the community pay "from

[2] Once the correlation between income and elasticity (i.e., "what the traffic will bear") is eliminated from the relationship, income itself no longer can predict the fees patients are charged.

five to thirty times the average fee."[3] Obviously the leader-
ship of the AMA must have a set of coercive devices to get
individual doctors to toe the line as price discriminators.
These devices include, among others, control over post-
graduate medical training and admission to speciality exam-
inations as well as control over hospital-use rights.

For instance, it is the AMA which determines, via certifi-
cation, which hospitals are allowed interns. By controlling
this supply of low-cost, trained hospital personnel, the AMA
has induced hospitals to employ only members of county
medical associations.

A doctor who cuts prices to higher-income patients soon
finds himself outside the door of his county medical association. He cannot then use hospital facilities for surgery, his
patients will not be admitted to hospitals, and his income
will fall accordingly. Moreover, a doctor must be a member
of his county medical association in order to take the exam-
inations for various high-paying specialities. If he chooses to
rebel, he promptly loses his county medical membership (or
is not allowed to join if he is new), and consequently his
potential career as a specialist is blocked.

4. It should now be more obvious why the AMA opposes
only certain kinds of medical insurance plans: Some plans
do not allow price discrimination. Specifically, the AMA has
pitched battle against all group health plans that charge a
fee which is a function only of the number of participating
family members. The AMA does not fight Blue Cross–Blue
Shield because that plan allows the individual subscriber
to choose any doctor who is a member of the county medical association. Differential pricing according to patients'
income can thus be maintained. Certain attempts by the
AMA to destroy group health plans have been brought to
trial and defeated. For example, the District Medical Society
in Washington, D.C., along with the AMA, was prosecuted
under the Sherman Antitrust Act in 1943 when it attempted
to put Washington Group Health out of business.

[3] H. Cabot, *The Doctor's Bill* (New York: Columbia University Press, 1935),
p. 270.

5. When we keep in mind the above facts, the remarkably high costs of Medicare should not be surprising. Doctors practice price discrimination. Before Medicare existed, indigent patients were charged relatively little for medical services. When their "income" potential increased they (that is, Medicare) were charged higher prices. The insurance industry has documented evidence that doctors do, in fact, charge "all the traffic will bear" and Medicare has made that tolerance higher.

Furthermore, Medicare statistics provide additional empirical evidence that much of the demand for health services is not as inelastic ("critical," "essential," "absolutely necessary") as people have been led to believe. Because the price to the buyer fell drastically when Medicare was instituted, the quantity demanded responded accordingly.

6. We cannot have "free medical care, as in Britain" for one simple reason: Free medical care does not exist, not even in Britain. The British are merely paying for it indirectly, through drains on tax revenues, instead of directly, via individual patients settling accounts with individual doctors. Any service that requires the use of resources—i.e., doctors' time, nurses' time, and hospitals—costs something. The U.S. could socialize medicine, but we would still have to pay the opportunity costs of all services received. If the supply of doctors were still controlled by the AMA and the government regulated their pay scale, we might end up with *less* medical care than now, for there would be even fewer doctors around.

This last statement does not constitute an argument against socialized medicine. With adequate salary incentives, we could have as many doctors as required. Socialization of medicine would, in fact, allow low-income people (actually *all* people) to obtain medical care that they might not have chosen to spend their money on if they were forced to pay for it. More people would be induced to undergo medical care because the costs would be borne indirectly by the whole community, instead of individually. If society feels this is a desirable goal, then socialization of medicine is a possible course of action.

There are alternatives to socialization, of course, including a nationwide insurance plan. But whichever of the several feasible methods might be chosen, the basic point for consideration is that once health care is made "free" to all, the quantity demanded will shoot upward. If enough doctors and hospitals are available,[4] then the problem is merely how to pay for all of the "free" services. But, of course, it should be obvious that whatever plan is adopted, those who are healthy will end up subsidizing those who are less healthy.

[4] Probably an impossibility, as long as the AMA controls the supply of M.D.s.

10

THE ECONOMICS
OF RISK AND INSURANCE

In the summer of 1970, Palestinian guerrillas skyjacked a Boeing 747 and blew it up. While reporting the incident, a radio announcer stated, with obvious relief, that "fortunately the 747 was fully insured." Are we to believe, then, that the loss of $25 million for the "jumbo jet" represented no loss at all since the airline company that owned it, Pan Am, was fully reimbursed? By now you should be aware of the fact that nothing is "free." Society paid the opportunity cost of that dynamited jet. True, the airline company suffered no loss, but the same cannot be said for the insurance firm that had to shell out the $25 million; in fact, all concerned ended up paying for the loss of the jet. To understand how and why, we must examine the economics of insurance and risk, and the industry associated with spreading risk via insurance.

Everyone knows that life is not a stable path to the Promised Land. We all face the vagaries of chance. Fire can strike our houses. Accidents can destroy our cars. Robbery can leave us without valuable possessions. And many things can cause our premature deaths. If enough people wish to reduce the risks involved in certain aspects of living, they can pool their risks together, so that for the entire group the probability of, say, one person's house burning up is small and predictable. It is predictable if data for the group have been collected long enough to provide an average estimate of house-burnings per year for specific groups of houses.

Insurance companies spend much of their resources in estimating the frequency of loss-causing events for specific groups and locations. When such estimates are obtained, an insurance premium can be calculated by the company. It takes into account the frequency of a particular event, like house fire, and also the loss payment which must be made to compensate the person or business which suffers the loss. Obviously, for the insurance company to make a profit, it must have good data for its estimate. It must charge higher insurance premiums when losses occur more frequently and also for higher-value losses. When a new technological invention, such as a $30 million communications satellite, is put into use, insurance companies have no idea what the probability of failure is. They have few means for assessing the premium. Of they were to take a guess and were proved wrong in the "wrong" direction, it would mean financial disaster.

Insurance-company premiums also include a "load factor" which is designed to cover the administrative costs of running the business.

Insurance companies have been insuring airplanes for many years. They have charged the airlines a premium which took into account the average number of crashes per year for all planes and the cost of replacing destroyed planes. Then along came skyjacking and dynamiting. Insurance companies suddenly found that their profits were destroyed by the unexpected demolition of a very costly 747 (and a few 707s to boot). The previous estimates used to calculate premiums were no longer valid. The probability of plane destruction had suddenly skyrocked. The dynamiting of the jumbo jet not only ended up costing the insurance company $25 million, but it also resulted in the drying up of some money for insuring today's jets. It turned out that the potential loss to the insurer had become so high and the increased probability of loss so large due to skyjacking, that few companies felt they could make enough profit in the deal. U.S. airlines were forced to set up their own insurance company to cover that part of their losses that regular companies would no longer insure. And, of course, the rates on those losses still insured have gone up. Air fares for all will consequently be higher in the future. It's fortunate for Pan American Airways that their 747 was insured, but all those concerned with airlines are ending up paying for that disaster.

The same is true of the increasing rate of automobile accidents and the increasing costs of auto repairs. The loss estimates that insurance companies use to establish their most profitable premiums have been changing, and auto insurance rates have consequently gone up. The auto insurance industry is highly competitive, and few will maintain that these firms are making monopoly profits. With this in mind, what do you think happens in states that put a ceiling on auto insurance rates? Given that insurance firms are making no more than a competitive rate of return to start with, the imposition of a ceiling on rates in the face of rising costs leads to the cancellation of coverage to all high-risk drivers or the refusal of the insurance companies to issue any insurance in those states with ceiling rates. Firms will not usually continue any aspect of business if they cannot make a normal profit.

At the same time that auto rates in general have been rising, the rates for certain classes of drivers and cars have been falling. The explanation lies in the competitive nature of the insurance industry. Each firm desires more business. One way to attract it is to lower price. To find out where they could *profitably* lower rates, companies have continually searched the data on specific groups of people and cars to find out where the probability of accidents was lowest. Hence we find that compact cars are insured for a smaller premium because data have shown insurance companies that these types of vehicles are involved in less costly accidents. Young people who have passed a driver-training course pay less for insurance because data have shown that they are involved in fewer accidents.

Insurance is one way of providing for disaster, one way of spreading risk among many people at a relatively low cost to each one. But we have devised other ways of doing this. If you wish a relatively riskless future income from your savings, you can buy U.S. government bonds, which rely on the taxing power of the state for their repayment. The interest and principle on these bonds are without risk of default. If you want a little higher income with somewhat more risk, you can purchase grade Aaa corporate bonds. At the other end of the risk scale you can buy highly speculative over-the-counter stocks which may yield you no income in the future, or even the loss of your entire investment, but with the small probability of a very large gain.

People can even choose how much risk they want in their regular income. A federal bureaucratic job offers little risk of termination, but also little chance of a large income. A stab at Hollywood offers a large risk of no employment and no income with the possibility of a large income if success strikes.

In sum, people can within limits choose among a vast array of different combinations of risk and income, both in their jobs and in the preservation of their assets through the purchase of various types of insurance policies. But no one can completely avoid all risk. We said that U.S. government bonds were *relatively* riskless because the holder knows he will always be paid off. But even these assets are not *completely* riskless because their value can be eaten away by inflation. Let's take a simple example. You buy a $1,000 bond when there is no inflation. The coupon rate of return is 4 percent; that is, each year you send in a little coupon to the U.S. Treasury and they send you a check for $40. Everything goes along well for a few years. Then all of a sudden the general level of prices starts going up. Let's say that, by the time you get the principal back on your bond, prices in general have increased 30 percent over what they were when you bought the bond. Your $1,000 will be worth only $700.

Now, it is true that if you expected the inflation to happen you never would have paid $1,000 for the bond to start with. For example, if you expected a 3 percent rate of inflation every year, you would have paid only enough to yield you the 4 percent you would get with the coupons *plus* an inflation factor or 3 percent. So you would actually only pay that amount which would make the $40 the U.S. Treasury sent you every year equal to about 7 percent of the purchase price of the bond. However, the minute inflation goes over 3 percent per year, you will again lose out. Similarly, if it goes below 3 percent per year, you'll gain.

No matter what path one takes in life, risks are involved. They can be minimized but never eliminated completely.

11

THE ECONOMICS
OF THE DRAFT VS.
AN ALL-VOLUNTEER ARMY

For more than a decade Congressmen have been proposing legislation to replace the draft with an all-volunteer army. For more than a decade their proposals have been shot down as unrealistic and, above all, too expensive, especially in time of war.

The draft has been with us for almost two centuries, being first instituted during the War for Independence. Massachusetts and Virginia used conscription in 1777. On February 6, 1778, Congress recommended that the other colonies follow suit, but because France sent troops it was unnecessary to initiate a general draft.

In April 1862 the Confederacy started universal conscription. By 1863 the North saw fit to pass the Enrollment Bill. During the Civil War, however, men who were conscripted were allowed to "buy" someone else to go in their stead. Therefore, even though the method of conscription was arbitrary, the final determination of who would go to war was more flexible. For example, a lawyer who found himself conscripted had the option of paying someone else to replace him. As long as the price he paid was lower than the amount he could earn by remaining at work, both parties benefited financially from the arrangement. Since many workers did not earn as much as a lawyer could (that is, their opportunity costs were lower) it was not hard to find a replacement at a mutually agreeable price. Quite understandably, relatively few of the fighting men in the Civil War came from higher-paying civilian occupations. Since a man's contribution to the economy can be roughly indicated by his salary, it can be said in economists' terminology, that an *efficient*[1] *allocation of resources* resulted, since men worked (or fought) where their services were of most value.

To detour for a moment into a fuller discussion of this question of allocation of resources: Inefficiency exists whenever men and machines are being used in such a manner that their full potential to the output of the economy is not being realized. A change from an inefficient to an efficient allocation therefore results, by definition, in an increase in output. This does not mean that everyone will be better off. All changes in our economy carry certain costs, and those who incur these costs are worse off. But in theory the increase in output allows those who bear the costs of the change to be fully compensated, assuming, of course, that some institutional mechanism exists by means of which the compensating "side payment" can be carried out.

To return now to the historical question of America's army-building techniques: During World War I, the form of conscription became a pure lottery, and draftees were not allowed to hire replacements. This method was altered somewhat during the World War II and the Korean War. From the Civil through the Korean Wars, a total of 14,448,330 men were inducted. Essentially the same economic analysis applies to all these men in all these conflicts and to those in Indochina today. Let's now consider certain economic aspects of the draft.

Costs that often go unnoticed are associated with any method of involuntary conscription. To simplify the explana-

[1] The term "efficient" as used in economics does not have any connotation of "good," "desirable," or "best," but merely refers to the most productive use of available resources.

tion, let us analyze the military as though it were a business, referring to "managers" who hire and fire "workers" and who allocate part of their fixed yearly budget to pay for machines instead of men. When the Army obtains soldiers at a wage rate lower than that which would induce these men to join of their own free will, the military managers are obtaining incorrect information about the true costs of their operation. When labor is artificially underpriced (because of the draft), military management ends up using fewer machines and more men than they would otherwise have done. Why? The decision is made along the following lines. At a given price for men, the Army must consider the possibility of adding machinery either to aid the men or to replace them in certain jobs. If an additional adding machine will allow one man to do the work that two men would have done without the machine, management must look at the relative prices in order to decide rationally if the machine should be rented (or bought). If one man costs $100 a week and one adding machine rents for $25, the machine will be used. But if the price for the man falls to $20 a week, it is not economically worthwhile to rent a machine for the purpose of saving manpower. Because draftees are, in fact, paid far below their "going price" on the labor market, or the price that would induce them to volunteer, we know that the military is using "too many" men. We may say, then, that conscription results in a higher than optimal men/machine ratio in the military. As we will see later, this inevitably costs society more resources than are necessary for any desired level of national defense.

Another added cost results from the fact that conscription is typically for a period of only two years. In all likelihood, if the military were composed entirely of volunteers obtained in the same way that firms hire their workers (adequate wages), the turnover time would be longer than two years. In fact, since the Army would certainly be paying much higher wages than those currently offered, its management would make every effort to insure that turnover time was substantially longer than presently.

Turnover involves very real costs. When a soldier comes

into the service, he is "green" and must be trained. Training involves the use of resources such as machines and other men's time. When the draftee's two years are up, someone else must be trained to fill his spot, at more cost.

In addition to the relatively high turnover costs associated with the draft, conscription also results in an inefficient allocation of men's talents once they are in the Army. In the civilian world one rarely sees college-trained men washing dishes and cleaning outhouses. Employers benefit from placing men where their training adds to productivity—that is, where they contribute most to the output of the firm. Not so in the Army.

All draftees are obtained at the same price, whether they are Ph.D.s or functional illiterates. As in business, incentive probably exists for military management to use draftees most effectively, but the signals are not as apparent as in the civilian world where the highly differentiated salaries of different-quality workers are unmistakable. To hire a Ph.D., an entrepreneur must pay more than he pays for an unschooled worker. It behooves the employer to get the most for his money by putting the Ph.D. to work at a task where he is most productive.

Another problem faces military management. As an inducement to volunteer, the Army offers a prospective soldier his choice of training schools. Volunteers, therefore, fill most of the available slots in these schools. The result, to give one example, may be that a previously unskilled man (who volunteers) is trained as a radio repairman, whereas a draftee already trained as an electronics technician is put to work at some simple job where his skills are wasted.

In addition to above costs, the economy suffers an opportunity cost for every man drafted that is *totally independent of what draftees are paid in the Army*. The true cost to society of a draftee is what he could be earning as a civilian. When a man is paid $10,000 by an employer, we can usually assume that the employer is obtaining at least that amount in services; otherwise he would terminate the arrangement. If the same man is drafted, the economy is giving up about $10,000 worth of civilian productive services a year to obtain a much smaller amount in military services. *That* amount, and not the $1,500 in Army pay he will receive, is the true annual cost of his induction.

Since the Army pays (via tax dollars) only a small fraction of the true opportunity cost of draftees, who, then, pays the rest? Obviously, the draftees themselves bear the burden of an implicit tax which roughly equals the difference between their civilian pay and their Army pay.[2] But we all suffer somewhat, because the output of nonmilitary goods and services is lower and more expensive because these men are not working at their civilian jobs (unless, of course, all draftees are taken from the ranks of the unemployed).[3]

Examination of the distribution of this implicit tax discloses that the current draft system is highly favorable to the rich and highly unfavorable to the poor, mainly because of all the exemptions available to higher-income draft candidates. It is actually a highly *regressive tax,* in that the higher the income level, the lower the tax paid, on the average, measured as a percentage of income. Exemptions for those attending college and graduate school, which preceded the recent lottery system, merely amplified the regressive effects. What proportion of the poor and of minority races continue their education past high school? Even under the lottery system, the rich have resources to call on: lawyers, doctors, and psychiatrists to help them avoid the draft. In 1969, of 283,000 men drafted only 28,500 were college men. This figure represents 10 percent of the total drafted, whereas in the total male college-age population of the United States 40 percent are in college. The end to college deferments has therefore lessened, but not cured, the regressive effect of the "draft tax."[4]

[2] To the Army pay should be added the benefits of training and education obtained while in the service, plus any consumption value received ("Join the Army and see the world").
[3] Some say we benefit because military service "makes men out of boys," good citizens out of bad, and community leaders out of juvenile delinquents. Of course, there may be cheaper ways of obtaining these "goods."
[4] Note that the lottery may be even less efficient than the draft with exemptions, because with the draft those men whose contribution to civilian output is high do not get drafted. This does not, of course, mean that exemptions are "good."

What would happen with an all-volunteer Army? First, for the proposal to become a reality, the pay of soldiers would have to be raised until the requisite enlistment was reached without any conscription. Given that level, we could predict that: (a) the ratio of men to machines would decrease; (b) turnover rates would fall, together with all the associated costs; and (c) soldiers would be placed where their skills would contribute the most to the military—that is, in economic terms, where the value of their marginal product was highest.

It should be obvious by now that it is *not* true that an all-volunteer army would cost "too much." It would cost less in actual productive resources used because of the three points just mentioned. The real cost of an army is the opportunity (alternative) cost of all the men and machines it uses. Society pays this no matter what. The decision to have, or not to have, a volunteer army is really a decision about who should bear that cost. At present the economic burden is shared in small part by the taxpayers and in great part by the draftees. With a volunteer army only the taxpayers would pay the costs because there would be no draftees.

There still remain numerous noneconomic aspects of this question which we have no special competence to treat. Many potentially valid criticisms of both the draft and its alternatives must be considered. These include the contentions that a professional Army would have too much independent power and that an all-volunteer Army would end up composed only of the black and the poor.

Economics is silent before questions of this sort. It tells only the price that must be paid, and by whom, under one system or the other.

12
THE ECONOMICS
OF BASEBALL, BASKETBALL,
AND FOOTBALL

The reserve clause is "reasonable and necessary" to maintain the stability of the game. So ruled Federal Judge Irving Ben Cooper in the summer of 1970. His ruling went squarely against baseball player Curt Flood's antitrust suit. Flood's case seems little more than the first inning in a long game with the courts (according to his lawyer Arthur Goldberg), but we can at this time make an economic analysis of why the reserve clause is favored by baseball-team owners, and what the effects will be if it is ever declared illegal.

The reserve clause binds a player to work exclusively for the team which holds his contract; the player can be traded to another team without his permission. If he does not like his salary or working conditions, his only option is to quit the game altogether.

To gain perspective, let us look first at a labor market which has no reserve clause: the market for gardeners. Most gardeners charge what they think is the "going" price for their services. If one charges considerably less than this price, some potential additional customers will eventually find out. He will then find himself with many new requests for his services. If he is not willing to put extra hours into gardening, he will have to decide on one, or a combination, of the following courses: (a) he can lower the quality of his service so that each job requires less time, and he can squeeze in more customers; (b) he can refuse the additional work; (c) he can raise his prices so that certain customers, present or potential, will not be interested in obtaining his services. Obviously the first choice is equivalent to the third one, since a change in quality at the same price exerts the same economic effect as a change in price for the same quality.

On the other hand, if a gardener who does not have enough work wishes to attract more customers, he is free to lower his price or raise the quality of his services. That is, gardeners can compete among themselves to maximize their own individual incomes. To be sure, not all gardeners do this.

Now let's assume that a particular gardener gains a reputation for doing exceptionally good work. If he already has a full schedule, a potential customer will have to offer some incentive to gain his services on a regular basis. An adequate incentive might persuade the gardener to do one of the following: (a) work more intensively, (b) work longer hours and take fewer holidays, (c) drop one of his former customers.

The usual form of inducement is an offer of higher wages, although the award might be nonmonetary. In any case, by employing such tactics people desiring to obtain gardeners' services are competing among themselves. Although not all homeowners take the trouble to find out which gardener in the neighborhood gives the best service at the lowest price, some do.

We have just described the workings of a competitive market in gardening. The gardeners are free to vary the price, quantity, and quality of the service they sell. Homeowners are free to vary the price (wage) they offer, and the quantity and quality of service they demand. Theoretically, gardeners end up getting a wage that just equals the value of their services (i.e., they are paid the value of their marginal product). Buyers of gardeners' services end up just paying for the opportunity cost of these services, no more, no less (i.e., they must pay the value of the gardeners' marginal product).

What would happen if all homeowners in the country got together and decided to institute a "gardening reserve clause?" The reserve clause would require that each individual gardener work for only one homeowner (or, more realistically in this case, for one group of owners). The gardener could not work anywhere else unless the owner of the contract with the reserve clause decided that he, the owner, wanted to sell or trade the contract. Notice that one crucial aspect of the previously described competitive market has been eliminated: Gardeners cannot seek out the most advantageous job opportunities or compete for business, because only the homeowners can initiate a move. It is surely apparent that such restraint would prevent gardeners from seeking employment that would maximize their income and that it could leave them worse off than they were under free and competitive conditions.

They not only could but most certainly *would* be worse off if all homeowners then got together to form a cartel with the express agreement that they would not compete among themselves for gardeners' contracts. Competition in the gardening market would be stifled on both sides: among the sellers of gardening services and among the buyers of those services.[1]

What is pure hypothesis in our example has become stern reality in the world of baseball. Within the major leagues, teams have made up an interlocking set of agreements among themselves which yields a very special players' contract. Since the terms include an agreement not to tamper with a player "reserved" by any team, the contracting club in effect holds a unilateral option on the player's services for the following year. Once the player signs he must accept

[1] Of course it is hard to imagine a cartel of so many people actually working. The incentive to cheat would be too great, the problem of inducing new homeowners to join would be large, and the cost of enforcement of the agreement would be tremendous.

all the agreements made between teams; therefore, his only course is to attempt to get the highest salary possible from his particular team with no help from other competing teams. His choice is simple: to accept the offered salary or not to play baseball—at least not with any United States major league team.

The reserve clause allows a baseball team to restrain the workings of the job market for baseball players. Therefore, a monopoly element enters into baseball hirings.[2] Baseball teams contend that the reserve clause is essential to the game because it allows for an even distribution of good players among all teams. It is asserted that without the reserve rules richer clubs would bid away all the best talent. Games would be lopsided, and bored spectators would quit buying tickets.

Although plausible at first glance, this argument loses validity when it is realized that any industry could make a similar statement. In practice rich firms do not buy up all the best workers and thus make the manufacturing "game" lopsided. Firms and baseball clubs can always borrow money to invest in good workers and good players if the potential payoff from doing so is high enough. Obviously, if only one good (rich) team existed, the payoff from building a competing good team would be high enough to allow a club to borrow money (or sell additional stock) in order to do so.

The Sherman Antitrust Act specifically forbids action in restraint of trade, but the Supreme Court ruled in 1922 that owners of baseball teams were exempt from such federal legislation; the ruling was upheld in 1953. Whether it will be upheld again when Curt Flood's case finally gets to the Supreme Court is uncertain. The economic analysis is not.

The reserve clause is an attempt to restrict competition among teams for players. Hence, players are making less money now than they would without the reserve clause.

Take the example of Curt Flood. He is one of the highest-paid players in baseball; yet his average annual earnings from 1956 to 1969 were $11,889. Moreover, his expected

---

[2] The technically correct term is *monopsony*—one buyer.

career life is limited to 20 years. In contrast, more than half of the self-employed professionals in the U.S. were making over $15,000 in 1967, and their expected career life is 40 years. In arguing his case in court, Curt Flood's attorney made the point that the reserve system tends to depress players' wages. The data adequately support the assertion.

It might appear that competition among teams to sign newcomers could eliminate some of the exploitation of players. For a while "side payments" to new players did serve this end, but now a draft system has been inaugurated under which no such payments are allowed.

The impact of the reserve clause on players' salaries was, for quite some time, augmented by the effects of a compact between the National and American leagues *not* to compete for each other's players. Such an arrangement obviously would suggest the potential for a third league to bid the best players away from the other two by offering higher salaries. No third U.S. league could have succeeded, however, because players who might have signed with it would be forever barred from the American and the National leagues. Apparently not enough players were willing to take this chance, and no other major league appeared.

Baseball is not the only sport in which team owners have attempted to keep the wages of players below their competitive level. For 22 years basketball had only one professional league; then, in 1967, the American Basketball Association was formed. Not surprisingly, basketball players were, until recently, getting the lowest pay of all professional team athletes. A reserve clause exists in basketball, but it was effective only as long as the National Basketball Association was unchallenged. When the ABA was formed, players' salaries skyrocketed.

Recently the two professional basketball leagues have tried to merge. The move has been temporarily blocked by an injunction granted the NBA players' association, but the Court has allowed the leagues to seek a Congressional blessing on the merger.

Professional football is almost the image of professional baseball. There was only one league, the NFL, from 1919 until 1960, when the AFL appeared. Players' salaries prompt-ly shot upward manyfold.

When the National Football League ruled the scene, teams could "draft" players and that was it. No competition by larger salary offers was allowed. The players were thus pre-vented from maximizing their incomes by a collusive agree-ment among NFL team owners. And there was no competing league to bid players away.

In 1966, after 6 years of "competition," the AFL and NFL agreed to merge. Congress approved the move as a rider to a public housing bill![3] This merger has affected the free-dom of players. Although the terms state that after playing out his contracts' 1-year option the player may sign with any other team, that team has to compensate the one he left. This may be, of course, discouraging to the second team. The player can also attempt to arrange a trade through the offices of the Football Commissioner, but the results to date have not been very favorable to the players involved. The AFL–NFL merger, by precluding the need to compete for players, has obviously held the salaries of players lower than they would have been under freely competive conditions.

The situations described above do not necessarily indicate that team owners in professional sports actually planned along the lines of our analysis. Yet they need not have done so for our thesis to prove valid. We have provided a theory of collusive behavior with some obvious implications about players' salaries. The validity of the implications is borne out by the facts.

[3] This, in spite of a 1967 court ruling that football was subject to anti-trust laws.

13

THE ECONOMICS
OF THE AUTOMOBILE

Between 1940 and 1970 the number of automobiles in the United States has increased from 22 million to 106 million, so that today the ratio of automobiles to people is 1 to 2. The automobile has probably done more to transform American society in the twentieth century than has any other technological invention. It has become thought of as a "necessity," an essential ingredient in our way of life. It has also become the chief scapegoat in a vast array of modern problems such as air pollution, urban decay, congestion, and noise pollution. The automobile itself is not the culprit, however; if left alone it would cause only crowded garages. The guilty party creating all these problems is the automobile *owner* who bears only the private costs of operating his vehicle while shrugging aside the social costs that mount with every mile he drives.

When there is a divergence between *social costs* and *private costs,* we say that an *externality* exists. Costs external to the private decision-maker are not included in his calculations. In many cases an externality occurs because of the inability of all concerned to arrange a contractual agreement that would eliminate the problem. People adversely affected by your automobile exhaust cannot easily contract with you to eliminate the problem. So you go driving about without considering the social cost.

The automobile owner's private costs are his monthly loan payments, operating costs, and annual license fees. Included in operating costs are insurance and federal and state taxes on gasoline. Yet, each automobile owner imposes costs on society which greatly exceed his private costs. Let's see what the true social costs are.

Automobiles are responsible for approximately 60 percent of the air pollution we breathe. Cars pour 230,000 tons of carbon monoxide into our air every day. In Los Angeles, auto exhaust accounts for about 90 percent of the pollution.

Every time a driver enters a crowded freeway he contributes to the congestion, causing other drivers to arrive at their destinations just a little later. At rush hours everyone tries to use the freeways at the same time, with the result that no one goes anywhere. Each driver is therefore imposing a cost on every other driver. And what does our one motorist contribute to this nightmare? His contribution is the sum of the marginal costs in extra time imposed on all other drivers by his presence. If we value each driver's time as equal more or less to his wage rate (opportunity cost), then the social cost any one driver levies with respect to congestion is considerable.

As he drives down the road, a driver is also contributing to the noise that envelops the highway, and he is thus piling up more social costs. What would be the value of noise abatement, and what is the marginal contribution of each driver to the total of noise? Like so many problems involving social vs. private costs, these are difficult questions. Perhaps values can be assigned only by determining how much the populace would be willing to pay to avoid this form of pollution.

"Visual pollution" is another social cost imposed by America's automobiling populace. The eye is offended by abandoned cars littering the roadsides, by junkyards of crumpled vehicles, and only slightly less by the 230,000 gas stations that stand shoulder to shoulder across the national landscape.

The real problem with these externalities is to find a valid measure of the social cost in each case and to discover an effective way to assess each driver according to his just share. This is not an impossible task. We are gradually discovering ways of isolating and imposing, if not the total social cost, at least enough of it to encourage the originator of the externality to alter his behavior.

Suppose, for example, that the goal is to eliminate the externalities caused by congestion in city streets. For a tollway, it is easy to impose charges that take account of all costs because the exits and entrances are relatively few. But how could city streets be metered effectively? A technological solution was suggested some years back by Professor William Vickrey, but it met with little success. He proposed that TV cameras be installed at those intersections where heaviest congestion occurred. It would then be possible to record the license numbers of all cars using these intersections at rush hours and to store the information in a computer. At the end of each month, motorists would be sent a bill for all the times they drove in the metered intersection.[1] To be sure, some motorists would avoid areas where metering devices were installed, but this would be all to the good. Motorists would then be driving in uncongested parts of the city or finding an alternative means of transportation.

When congestion occurs, many drivers are prevented from entering the city. These "losers" are not, at present, compensated in any way by those motorists who cause the congestion. What's more, motorists cannot be paid *not* to use the streets so as to reduce congestion.

---

[1] Another alternative suggested by Vickrey was the use of the Oxford electronic metering device, triggered by radio signals, since each passing car would emit a unique signal. Either procedure, however, raises the critical problem of invasion of privacy, since data stored in the computer could conceivably be released to other agencies.

The reader can perhaps see now that the problems created by automobile drivers are in principle solvable if we can impose an increasing share of the social cost of the automobile on its owner. Motorists will then have an incentive to pressure producers to devise cars that are quieter and free of pollutants. If we can measure the pollution emitted by an engine and the noise a car generates, ways can be found to impose an appropriate tax on each owner. If tolls are levied on major access roads and varied according to rush hours, traffic congestion and peak-load problems can be reduced. If penalties are imposed for abandoned cars or rewards paid for turning them in, and if suitable penalties are laid on junkyards for pollution, the landscape will be improved.

One predictable obstacle to all such innovation is the political furor of the American motorist. His devotion to his own, private mode of transportation is well documented and is pointed up by the dilemma of urban mass-transit systems. From the New York subway to the Seattle bus system, these have one thing in common: They lose money.

Proposed solutions have been many. In the San Francisco Bay area, BART is busily developing an integrated rapid-transport network. Other areas are raising or lowering prices, depending upon whether authorities view the demand as inelastic or elastic at existing prices. In Flint, Michigan, passengers have been enticed by a fleet of luxury buses complete with air conditioning, stereophonic music, and in some cases even a Bus-Bunny to handle complaints (if any). The allurement failed. According to the *Wall Street Journal* (September 4, 1969), the so-called "Maxicabs" were each losing about $200 a day.

Given the present costs of driving a car, most people obviously prefer their own faithful vehicle, no matter how battered it may be. And that is to say that no system of public transportation, however sexy, can succeed as long as users of private cars are exempt from bearing a greater share of the real costs they impose upon society. Moreover, the demand for automobile transportation is probably income elastic, so that as incomes rise over time an even greater share of commuters will use their own cars instead of public transportation.[2]

If each driver were to be charged the true social cost for his vehicle, he would have to shoulder his share of the burden for air pollution, noise pollution, and any congestion caused. Even if manufacturers were able to develop engines which would virtually eliminate exhaust pollution (at a cost to the buyer of the car, of course) the remaining charges would still be substantial—for noise and especially for congestion. The most critical element in congestion is the peak-load problem of commuter traffic in and out of the city during rush hours. The freeways and roads are filled to capacity for only a few hours each day; but to cope with this differential, designers must plan for the peak-load stresses. All taxpayers pay for the additional capacity built in for these short periods. A charge imposed on peak-load users would result in a reduction in traffic at those times.[3] Commuters would then have an incentive to pool rides, to utilize the much cheaper, even if somewhat less convenient, alternative of rapid transit, or to drive during uncongested hours when the charge for use would be zero.

Until some such incentive is developed, we repeat, large-scale investment in rapid transit is likely to prove a losing proposition. We will be forever saddled with a society centered around the horseless carriage and the problems it has sired.

[2] This statement implicitly assumes that the relative costs of motoring do not change. Of course, as congestion increases, implicit motoring costs do rise and less quantity is demanded than otherwise.
[3] See also pp. 28–29.

14
THE ECONOMICS
OF OIL SPILLS

In March 1967 the oil tanker *Torrey Canyon* foundered off the southern coast of England, spilling 119,000 tons of crude oil. The resulting slick quickly spread across nearby waters and subsequently blanketed large areas of adjoining English and French coasts. The British government alone spent $8 million on cleanup; and that was only a portion of total cleanup costs. In addition, there was extensive loss of marine life and fouling of beaches and coastlines.

This disaster drew widespread attention because of the extent of the damage it caused. People were suddenly made aware of the threat posed by modern supertankers with capacities now ranging up to 300,000 tons. However, the *Torrey Canyon* catastrophe is only one spectacular example of a burgeoning problem. In 1967 a total of 2,353 ship accidents occurred. Of these 1,347 involved vessels which were over 1,000 tons, 499 involved tankers or tank barges, and 1,569 of these mishaps occurred in U.S. waters. Since most ships are typically fueled by oil, the threat of spillage is not limited to tank ships and barges. In addition to accidents, spills can also result from leaks in transferring oil, from the deliberate pumping out of bilges, and from blowouts of offshore wells, as in the Santa Barbara case.[1] Since oil is not biodegradable (does not deteriorate rapidly), the oceans of the world are accumulating an ever-increasing mass of "indigestible" petroleum; slicks and globules of oil are visible throughout the high seas of the world. The biological consequences are still indeterminate—we simply do not know what the long-run effects on marine life will be. But anybody who has walked the beaches barefoot has had no trouble discovering the fouling consequences on coastlines.

Some technological methods have already evolved for cleaning up the mess, and better ones can be devised in the future. But it may prove far less costly to society to effectively prevent future spills. Several alternatives can be considered.

One proposed solution is simply to prohibit offshore drilling and the transportation of petroleum products by water. This would certainly reduce oil spills, but it might lead to undesirable side effects for various sectors of the community. The short-run effects would be a reduction in the supply of crude oil and a resultant rise in the price of all petroleum products. Rich and poor alike use gasoline, but it represents a larger proportion of the expenditures of the poor.[2] Hence a greater burden would fall on low-income groups. The long-run consequences of such a policy are somewhat more difficult to determine. A rise in the price of petroleum products would increase the profitability of new domestic discoveries and thereby lead to more intensive exploration. Whether this would increase the supply sufficiently to cause the price to fall to earlier levels is not easily predicted.

Moreover, even such a drastic measure taken by the U.S.

[1] The focus of this chapter is on oil spills directly into water. An additional problem is posed by oil spills on land—intentional or accidental—from pipelines, disposal of used oil from 230,000 gasoline stations, etc. Eventually such oil seeps into streams, rivers, lakes, and oceans.
[2] Studies have shown the following distribution of gasoline expenditure as a proportion of income: $3,000–5,000 income, 3.4 percent; $5,000–7,000 income, 3.3 percent; $7,000–15,000 income, less than 2 percent; above $15,000, 1.4 percent.

would not completely solve the problem, because other nations' tankers would still carry oil and continue to foul the oceans. Since our legal authority extends only a short distance to sea, our beaches would still not be safe from wandering oil slicks.

It is clearly possible to eliminate most ecological problems by simply shutting off any economic activity which has costs to "innocent bystanders" *(external diseconomies).* But this is usually a prohibitively expensive solution. The number of economic activities with external diseconomies is constantly growing, and totally forbidding such activities would result in a drastic fall in living standards. Can we, then, eliminate the bulk of these side effects without eliminating the economic activity that produces them? These baneful effects exist for one reason: The individuals or groups who create the costs do not bear them. If the polluter had to bear the costs, it would be in his interest to eliminate as many as possible.[3]

In short, one pat answer to most pollution questions is to make the polluter pay. But to do so, we are going to have to alter property rights—that is, change existing laws about ownership. Rights to property must be revised to include the costs as well as the benefits of any attendant economic activity. To cite only two polluters, this would make motorists and pulp-mill operators liable for the air and water pollution they cause.

Implicit in such a course would be the problem of determining the true economic costs of the side effects of certain activities. For example, how is a price tag to be put on the destruction caused by pollution from a steel mill's smokestacks? In principle, a price can be figured out. But in practice the task is far from simple and is compounded by the problem of effectively assessing the cost against the actual polluter.

This latter point is particularly thorny in the case of oil spills, since the ocean (and frequently even the beaches) are

[3] It is easy for people to assert that *all* pollution should be stopped; but the economy will have less real income if the costs of total elimination of pollution exceed the benefits.

not private property. They are a *common-property resource,* which means that no one owns them, and that everyone can use them. If somebody did own them, he would do what any other property owner does when damaged; he would sue the polluter for the full extent of the damages. This points to one direction which public policy can take. State and federal laws and international agreements are necessary to make polluters liable.

However, if liability is limited, then the small tank barge may be discouraged from operating, while the owners of the 300,000 ton tanker will take their chances. Here's why. Say that liability for oil spills could not exceed $100,000. If a small 50,000 ton independent tanker spilled its load, it would probably be assessed this maximum limit, which could mean financial ruin or at least crippling losses for the company. But if a 300,000 ton supertanker from Atlantic Richfield were to break apart, the maximum liability assessment would be a far lighter penalty relative to the potential profits from that superload of oil. Under any given probability of foundering, the supertanker will sail because potential profits are large enough to warrant risking a spillage fine. The small, one-ship company has no such comfortable assurance. Therefore, in order for the laws to be effective against oil spills, they must contain unlimited liability clauses.

What would be the results of such laws? Oil carriers would be forced to carry insurance sufficient to cover damages. The high costs of such coverage would probably eliminate giant tankers from some enclosed waters such as Puget Sound or Chesapeake Bay where the potential liability from a major oil spill would be of immense magnitude. Insurance premiums would decline with improvements in safety devices designed to prevent accidental oil spillage. Operators would therefore be encouraged to install such measures. There would also be an incentive to improve the technology of cleaning up oil spills and thereby to reduce the costs of damages. The suggested program would undoubtedly raise the price of petroleum products to consumers, particularly because the current-model supertanker would have to be replaced by higher-cost transport.

Such state, national, and international legislation would not solve all the problems connected with oil spills. As in the cases of narcotics and crime (Chapters 3 and 22), one challenge must always be the detection and identification of the culprit. A "finder's fee" for reporting polluters might provide some assistance. The above suggestions point toward a solution common to many ecological dilemmas— property rights will have to be realigned if private and social costs (and benefits) are to coincide. As long as individuals, firms, or even governmental units can foist some of the costs of their actions onto others, they will be human enough to do so. But if reorganized property rights can force the polluter to bear the full costs of his actions, he will have every incentive to act responsibly.

THE ECONOMICS
OF STANDARD OIL

The folklore of wildcat oil prospecting has been with us at least since the days of the 1901 Lucas Gusher on Spindletop, near Beaumont, Texas, and is still seems dear to the hearts of many. Today's oil industry is a far cry from what it was in those days. In 1859 Edwin L. Drake, copying the techniques of salt-well drillers, went after the rock oil which, up to that time, had been considered merely a pollutant of many brine wells. He managed to recover 2,000 barrels of oil that year near Titusville, Pennsylvania. By 1950 that 2,000-barrel figure had jumped to almost 2 billion and by 1970 annual oil output reached the 4 billion-barrel mark.

Congress has seen fit to bestow special considerations on oil exploration, production, and distribution because of the "special" nature of the product and because of national security considerations. Economic analysis can tell us about the effects of the legislation passed for the oil industry. Again we leave to individual judgment the decision as to whether the results are "good" or "bad."

Government intervention has caused the importation of oil to be restricted since 1955, first voluntarily and then involuntarily. During the Eisenhower administration, powerful oil interests convinced the Chief Executive that our national security was threatened by the flooding of the domestic market with low-priced foreign petroleum products. The argument ran that since oil prices were falling, domestic entrepreneurs would have no incentive to invest in exploration for new home-based sources of petroleum. More and more reliance would be placed on foreign supply lines, and in time of war these supply lines might be severed, leaving the U.S. military without an adequate supply of oil. Our bombers, fighters, and ships would be left stranded and rusting.

In 1955 Eisenhower instituted the first voluntary program of restriction on oil imports. Since it did not work too well, a second voluntary program was initiated in 1957. When this, too, failed to curtail imports, the President issued, on March 10, 1959, a proclamation placing oil imports under mandatory controls, and the oil-import quota system became law.

Let's see how it works, whom it benefits, and what the ultimate results will be if it continues. To insure that the supply of relatively low-priced foreign oil does not force down the price of domestic oil, the Oil Import Administration each year determines the total quantity of crude oil that may be imported. Permission to import is granted to the various companies according to the average amounts of crude oil each imported in the years 1954, 1955, and 1956. Special tickets authorize the importation of a certain number of barrels of foreign oil.

Once obtained, these tickets for imported crude oil can be traded to other refineries in exchange for other petroleum products. It is easy to figure out why such trading takes place. A barrel of foreign crude oil sells for as much as $1 to $2 less than domestic crude. Given the choice, any domestic refinery would be willing to pay for the right to buy foreign crude at the lower price. Since the tickets cannot be bought and sold outright,[1] they are used as a medium of

[1] As of the summer of 1970 the Department of the Interior was considering the possibility of permitting outright sale of the tickets by companies which were alloted them.

exchange. Companies wishing to import crude oil and lacking authorization will pay implicitly as much as $1.50 for a ticket which gives the right to import one barrel of foreign crude oil.

The distribution of import quotas has typically followed the distribution of oil-company size. Since the tickets are each worth approximtaely $1.50, those big companies which formerly imported vast amounts of foreign oil have received (and continue to receive) tremendous windfall gains proportionate to their previous imports; medium-sized companies have enjoyed moderate gains; small companies have been left out in the cold.

Although the distributional aspects of the gains from oil imports may not seem equitable, the fact that the quota ticket can be traded does lead to the most efficient use of the available foreign oil. Why? Simply because the most efficient refineries (those that get the most output per dollar of costs) can afford to offer the highest prices for the tickets; therefore, they are the ones which in the end will import the most oil for refining purposes.

It has been estimated that the oil-import quota program has so far cost consumers roughly $5 billion a year, and that this figure will rise to $7 billion annually in 1975 and to $8 billion in 1980. This cost is borne in the form of higher prices for gasoline, heating oil, and petroleum products than would prevail if unrestricted imports of foreign crude were allowed. Who collects all this money? The stockholders of those companies that receive the tickets.

If the government wished to rid the program of this peculiar feature but still maintain the domestic price of oil at its current high level, it could impose a *tariff,* a set of taxes on oil imports. The tariff rates could be raised to such a level that the quantity now entering under the quota system would still be imported. The big difference, however, would be that the United States Treasury, instead of the stockholders of Standard Oil and other big petroleum concerns, would collect $5 billion or more annually. Then taxes could be lowered correspondingly without lessening governmental funds.

Besides keeping the price of oil in the United States artificially high, the oil-import quota system induces oilmen to find and extract more domestic oil than would be profitable in a completely unrestricted situation. (The suggested tariff system would have the same effect.) Since more oil is being extracted, more resources are being used in the domestic oil industry than would normally occur.

In addition to the incentive of artificially inflated prices, American oilmen are currently being induced to use still larger amounts of resources (men and machinery) than would otherwise be optimal because of such special tax stimuli as depletion allowances, full costing of dry wells, and capital-gains tax privileges.

Since the amount of oil found in each pocket is eventually going to be depleted by the pump over it, owners of producing wells can opt for a special tax program whereby they are allowed percentage depletion deductions when computing their taxes. To understand this practice, the reader should understand that when a businessman buys a machine, he is allowed to deduct from his income the cost of the depreciation on the machine each year. Hence he pays no tax on that amount of income. Similarly, an oilman deducts a percentage of the depletion of his oil well. Currently he can deduct 22 percent of the gross value of the oil at the wellhead, but before 1970 the figure was 27 percent. Let's see why an oilman would prefer this scheme to the regular cost-depreciation schedule applied by businessmen for depreciation of machinery.

Look at it this way. If you pay $1 million for a machine, the total depreciation you can claim will not exceed $1 million. On the other hand, if you have a well that cost you $1 million and you opt for percentage depletion, you may be able to deduct more than $1 million. Why? Simply because the 22 percent depletion allowance can be used every year, forever! The total amount depleted may far exceed the actual amount spent on digging the well.

Contrary to popular belief, though, it appears that even when oilmen could use the higher 27 percent depletion allowances legally in force before 1970, this tax provision did not lead to excessive use of resources in domestic oil.[2] It is only when the controversial percentage depletion is heaped on top of the other oil-industry tax advantages that the full story becomes clear.

In oil exploration, a fact of life is that not all the drilled wells end up as gushers. On average, approximately 80 percent of all drilled wells are dry. Since wet wells cannot be found without hitting some dry ones, the implicit cost of a wet well must also include the cost of a proportionate number of dry ones. That is, on average the true cost of finding *one* producing well in the U.S. also includes the cost of drilling *four* dry ones.

The Internal Revenue Service seems to think along somewhat different lines, however, since it permits the costs of *all* dry wells to be deducted from other income. If you are a rich doctor who is a partner in an oil-exploration syndicate, you can deduct your part of the dry-well costs from your doctoring income. If your marginal tax bracket is 70 percent, every dollar you spend for dry-well exploration ends up costing you only 30 cents. (Of course the same is true for any other legitimate "business" expense which can be entered on a tax return.)

In addition to the dry-well tax provision, exploration firms which sell wet wells are required to pay only the capital-gains rate on the difference between the selling price and the total calculated costs of the wet well. (Remember that the dry wells' costs have already been deducted from other income.)

The oil explorer gets a double benefit. He can use the lower capital-gains rate[3] on the income from selling his wet wells and still get the benefit of a higher kickback by applying the cost deduction of dry wells to his other income,

[2] See A. Harberger, "The Taxation of Mineral Industries," in Joint Economic Committee report, *Federal Tax Policy for Economic Growth and Stability* (Nov. 9, 1955), pp. 438–448.
[3] One-half of his marginal rate up to a maximum of 25 percent for capital gains less than $50,000, up to a maximum of 32½ percent for capital gains greater than $50,000.

which is necessarily taxed at a higher than capital-gains rate (by a minimum of 50 percent more).

Depletion allowances, full costing of dry wells off other income, and capital-gains concessions are not given to the oil industry at no cost to the economy. The end result of the tax gimmicks is an eager-beaver devotion of resources to domestic oil development, increasing their normal usage by a scale of 1½ to 2½ times what might have been expected. Whether this is what the United States really needs is a political question.

16
THE ECONOMICS
OF AIRPLANE STACKING

"Ladies and gentlemen, this is your Captain speaking. Approach control for La Guardia Airport has put us twenty-third in line for landing, so we'll be holding here for awhile. Just relax, the planes aren't stacked up too badly this evening; you should be deplaning in about an hour and a half. Thank you."

Only the neophyte air traveler is shocked by such words any more, for experience has taught most people who fly that circling around the airport for an hour before landing is the normal course of affairs for a commercial jet. What is the matter? Is ground control inefficient? Are the pilots too slow? The planes too big? Or, is it merely that we don't have enough airports? Although economics cannot answer all these questions (because some are technical), it can shed light on why the problem has become so acute today and what the real issues are.

Let's look at a typical afternoon at New York's La Guardia Airport. It is 3:30 in the afternoon and you are coming in for a landing in a two-seater private plane. Ground control puts you in the line-up and you wait. All those planes ahead of you are not only waiting but are also, in effect, the cause of your delay in landing. But when a Boeing 727 comes in to land *you* are making him wait (and so are all the others before you). The presence of your little Cessna 150 is imposing enormous costs on that 727.

First and most obvious are the costs of jet fuel and the extra wear and tear on the engines. Then there is the opportunity cost of the time for the pilot, copilot, and stewardesses. These costs combined add up to about $6.50 *per minute!*[1]

And that is not all. If a highly qualified economic consultant to Rockefeller is aboard that 727, his time (opportunity cost) may be worth $30 per hour or 50 cents a minute. Summed up, the value of everyone's time in the average jet comes to almost $5 per minute.[2] And what about all those people waiting on the ground?

By deciding to land your Cessna at La Guardia during the rush hour, you have imposed highly identifiable costs on the owners and passengers of the jet that came in after you. The marginal cost of this delay is over $11 per minute for that plane behind you.

To be sure, if the jet had come in before you it would have delayed your landing, but the marginal cost of your delay (fuel, your time, etc.) would average only $1.50 per minute for a two-seater Cessna.

For La Guardia Airport, if we take into account everyone's opportunity cost for waiting, all the fuel consumed, and so on, a jet landing during the busy hour of 3 to 4 p.m. imposes a marginal delay cost of almost $1,100 on all the aircraft and passengers that end up waiting behind it.

Now one of the problems comes into focus. At certain times of the day the capacity of a given airport for landings and takeoffs is greatly exceeded. Thus the airplanes are forced to queue up for the right to use the runway and facilities. This queuing is not free. As we have shown, it

---

[1] Alan Carlin and R. E. Park, "Marginal Cost Pricing of Airport Runway Capacity," *American Economic Review*, Vol. LX, No. 3 (June 1970), pp. 310*ff*.
[2] *Ibid.*

uses up resources of equipment, fuel, and time for which the opportunity cost is enormous. The Federal Aviation Agency estimates that in 1968 delay of air carriers at 240 airport terminals served by FAA towers amounted to 19 million minutes and cost the domestic air carriers $118 million!

Given the existing supply of airports, how could this situation be improved? One possibility is to induce airport authorities to act like many private firms which also face peak-load problems. Some nightclubs, for example, have "too much" business on the weekends, so they add a cover charge applicable only to those crowded periods. Such action can readily be interpreted as an inducement for customers to come in during less busy periods.

Airports could act similarly by raising the landing and takeoff fees for preestablished rush hours. This additional charge would induce some private plane owners and perhaps a few airlines to reschedule flights so as to avoid the peak "penalty" fee. On examination, this course seems logically sound because it gives to airlines and to private plane owners signals (differentiated prices by time of day) commensurate with the costs each imposes on other users of the airport facilities. A truly efficient set of peak "penalty" fees would reflect exactly the marginal costs each plane imposes on others. At La Guardia, for example, landing fees would be relatively high from 2 to 8 p.m. and practically zero from 11 p.m. to 7 a.m.

Would airlines and private plane owners respond to these new fees? The evidence says yes. In August of 1968 the minimum fee for landings and arrivals at La Guardia was raised from $5 to $25 for flights between 8 and 10 a.m. during the week and between 3 and 8 p.m. every day. Since airlines were already paying well above the minimum, they were not affected by the price increase. But small private planes were, and their use of the airport during these times appears to have fallen by about 40 percent.

Apart from the problems caused by airport facilities, which are publicly owned and operated, there are aspects of the airline industry itself that contribute to long waiting

times during peak periods. One of these involves the regulation of air fares.

At present all scheduled airlines must charge the same
regulated set of prices. Since they cannot compete on the
basis of price, they compete on the basis of the quality of
the services they offer, and this includes the desirability of
departure and arrival times. To keep their competitive position, airlines tend to schedule many flights at the most
desirable times; the result is that half-full jets are taking off
and landing at precisely the busiest times. If airlines were
allowed to compete also on the basis of price, they would
have an incentive to lower costs as a necessary preliminary
to lowering rates. Since the cost of flying a jet is practically
the same whether it is full or half empty, the logical course
would be to schedule fewer flights at a given period and to
fill each plane more nearly to capacity. The desirable result
would be, of course, not only lower cost per passenger but
less crowding at airports even without the imposition of
"penalty" fees for peak-load usage.

This last statement, of course, rests on the assumption that
reduced air fares (brought about by price competition)
would not cause an increase in demand for air travel so
great as to necessitate even *more* flights than now exist.
What it really implies is a low price elasticity for airplane
travel. If elasticity should prove greater than anticipated, a
small decrease in air fares might indeed induce a large increase in the quantity demanded.

All the newspaper projections about how many more
people are going to fly in the future are based on an implicit prediction that increasing population and increasing
incomes will cause people to demand more air travel *at the
same prices that exist today.* That is to say, the predictions
of future increases in demand for air travel assume a high
income elasticity but do not consider *price* elasticity. If income elasticity is high in the case of air travel, increases in
income will induce people to use airplanes more than they
do now even at the same prices; if it is low, the reverse
will be true.

Historically, we have witnessed rising incomes and population along with falling relative prices for air fare (both in time and money). Domestic air travel increased from 634 million passenger miles in 1939 to 60,590 million in 1966. We also see a greatly expanded use of airplanes for carrying freight. Planes now account for more than 50 percent of common carrier traffic, contrasted with a mere 2.3 percent in 1939. These facts point up the inevitable alternatives that airport authorities (and society) are facing:

1. To maintain airport facilities at their present level. Queuing will continue to increase until all available use time, 24 hours a day, becomes filled. Then it will be technically impossible to accommodate additional planes. At this point, some rationing method will become absolutely essential. Peak-load penalty fees might be imposed, or merely increased use fees, which would lead to higher air fares and subsequently to fewer passengers. Or rights to specific time-slots might be sold to the highest bidders.
2. To build additional airport facilities. These might be financed by higher taxes to users, as President Nixon has suggested. Facilities could conceivably be built fast enough to eliminate peak-load congestion problems, so that a passenger would rarely find himself stacked up over an airport.[3] But it seems more likely that airports will still face the problem to some extent and that first-come, first-served, queuing will have to be replaced by some form of rationing if the air traveler is ever to be confident of landing on time, all the time.

---

[3] This does not mean that the *optimal* situation is one with no peak loading.

17
THE ECONOMICS
OF CLAMMING
AND OTHER "FREE" GOODS

The razor clam (*Siliqua patula*) is a large bivalve from the *Solenidae* family that inhabits the ocean beaches of the Pacific Coast from California to Alaska. Once a major staple of the coastal Indian population, it is now a major prey of the white man escaping the city for the ocean beaches. (Cleaned, cut into steaks, dipped in batter, fried 2 minutes to the side, and served with a bottle of dry white wine, it is superb.)

These clams are dug on minus tides, and the beach area they inhabit is not, at least in the state of Washington, private property. Therefore, access is available to everyone, and the only costs of digging them are cut fingers and an occasional dunking in icy water. Nobody owns them; they are a common-property resource, a "free good." But this fact does not make clams any less subject to economic analysis than goods with price tags on them. A demand schedule exists for clamming. Like other demand schedules, it shows that more people will use more of the product at a low price than at a high one; and that how *much* more they use will depend on how elastic their demand is (that is, how responsive to a given change in price). When the price is zero, as in clamming, the amount used will certainly be much more than at any level of positive price. Again, how much more depends on the elasticity of the demand schedule.

We can also derive, hypothetically at least, a supply curve, although to discover positive prices we would have to envision private ownership of beaches and see how many clams would be offered by beach owners at various prices. The higher the price, the more would be offered. Presumably, if the price were right, the owner would incur costs of "cultivating" and protecting clam beds to increase their yield.

If a market situation existed, an equilibrium price and quantity could be established; but since a wide gap is inevitable between the amount demanded at zero price and the amount supplied at zero price, some device must ration the product. State authorities take on this task, by setting daily catch limits and closing certain seasons to clamming. Current regulations for the state of Washington allow noncommercial diggers to take eighteen clams a day on any ocean beach from September 16 to July 15. What we have described is unfortunately only a short-run solution. In the dim and distant past when the Pacific Coast was sparsely settled, no particular problem existed (in fact, no limit of season was set, since in those days even at a zero price the supply exceeded the demand).[1] But each year more and more people have more income for traveling to beaches and more leisure to devote to clamming. The result is that the demand keeps increasing, and each year happy clam hunters crowd the minus-tide beaches thicker than sand-fleas. In Oregon the clam-seeking camper sometimes faces lines as much as a mile long.

The supply may also increase if new beaches are opened

---

[1] By 1925, regulations did limit commercial harvesting of Washington razor clams to the months of March, April, and May. A well-trained clam digger can remove as much as half a ton of clams during one low tide, but there was no need then to restrict the season for noncommercial clam digging.

up or the State Fisheries Department attempts to cultivate more clams on existing beaches. But the increase can be only minimal, once all the beaches have been made accessible. The result must inevitably be more crowding and fewer clams, year by year. It is not a happy prospect.

The clamming story is repeated over and over again for recreational activities, and the same analysis applies. In the case of wilderness areas, the supply is actually decreasing rather than merely remaining constant. Fishing, hunting, and camping sites are overcrowded, although these have somewhat greater potential for expansion of supply.

What is being done to improve the situation? A price is charged for fishing and hunting, in the form of license fees, and more recently camping sites in parks are being "rented." In each case, however, the rates have been set so far below the equilibrium price which could balance quantities supplied with quantities demanded that they are not even close to resolving the issue. And each year it gets worse. Anyone wanting to test the proposition need only visit Yellowstone or Yosemite National Park in the summer.

Why are we content with a zero price for clamming, or with only a nominal fee for fishing? The answer is that the American people have long believed that such activities are a hereditary right, that they should be equally accessible to rich and poor alike, and that charging a fee favors the rich (which it certainly does). This argument prevails in the cases of clamming, fishing, and hunting, but not in the case of buying yachts and airplanes. The result is to artificially lower the price for a particular publicly owned commodity—clams —but not for all commodities. In effect, the public policy is saying that income should not be a factor in people's ability to clam or to fish, but that it can be one in buying golf clubs, TV sets, or airplanes. That is, in effect, a policy of selective income redistribution—a subject to be examined in the final chapters of this book.

As crowding, rationing, and queuing become more and more severe in such nonpriced or underpriced activities, it becomes a major issue to determine whether rationing by price or by quantity restriction is the better method. One alternative is to eliminate the common-property aspect of such resources. Another is for the government to set a price that approximates a market price. The final alternative consists of a variety of rationing devices to restrict quantity more and more rigidly.

18

THE ECONOMICS
OF "FREE" VS. PAY TV

Every time a bill or referendum to establish pay TV has threatened to come before a state legislature, movie-theater owners have been quick to mount an emotional campaign to "save free TV!" The appearance of Proposition 15 on the California ballot in 1964 was a good example of vigorous campaigning by both theater owners and area network stations, who fostered the measure designed to outlaw pay TV entirely. The sponsors of the measure raised a $2 million war chest and vehemently portrayed subscription TV as robbing people of their right to the free product.

Of course it should surprise no one that those involved with selling a product called movies in a theater would be less than happy about the introduction of a product called movies in the home. Although the two products are not identical, they probably are considered as interchangeable by many consumers.

It is interesting that theater owners also fought "free" TV when it first appeared. Quite evidently, more people would be going to movies had TV never come into being. But the particular grudge that theater owners feel against TV ("free"

or not) is really no different from the misery any other entrepreneur experiences when competition starts taking business away from him.

The propagation and distribution of television signals do,
however, raise some unique questions. When a station emits
a TV or radio signal for any regular ("free") program, anyone
with a standard set within a certain radius of the transmitter
can pick up the signal. It is literally impossible for the station to charge individual viewers for watching or hearing its
programs. Moreover, once the program signal is emitted,
there is no further cost to the station for letting any additional person receive it. That is, the marginal cost is zero.

Also, when you decide to turn your set on, you do not
take the picture away from any other viewer. That is, the
marginal cost you impose on other viewers is zero.

This situation is clearly different from that of most other
goods and services in our economy. If you decide to eat an
apple, no one else can eat that particular apple. If you have
someone repair your car, that particular repairman cannot
work on another car at the same time. In both instances you
must usually pay for the right to use the good or service,
for that is typically the only way to obtain it. Even if you are
not charged market value, the opportunity cost still exists;
no one else can use the product or service in question.

There is no opportunity cost for the marginal unit of TV
signal that someone receives when he decides to turn on
his set. The signals are *public goods,* goods whose marginal
cost for an extra user is zero once the good (or service) is
produced. Public goods have another special characteristic:
To monitor their individual use is normally impossible or
prohibitively expensive; therefore, it is not feasible to charge
for that use. It can be seen that, in addition to TV and radio
signals, national defense meets the specifications for public
goods, as do uncongested roads. Many public goods are
governmentally owned or subsidized or they could not continue to exist.

How, then, has standard TV managed to flourish without
subsidies? Stations merely changed a public good into a
semipublic good by tying the selling of advertising time to

the production of the signals. Private television exists in the U.S. because firms air commercials at certain times of the day and night. But since firms must pay for that privilege, it is evident why we have been putting quotes around the word "free."

A business will expend resources on advertising only if it is profitable; that is, if the (marginal) costs are covered by the resultant (marginal) revenues. The products of firms which advertise on TV differ from other products precisely because they are TV-advertised and because the cost of the ads is included, at least in the long run, in the price of the product. Free TV is therefore not free at all: You pay for it if you buy the products seen in the commercials. In a very real sense, purchasers of those products are subsidizing the television viewing time of those who do not buy but who watch TV.

On the other side of the coin, we see that this issue does not arise with pay TV, for pay TV is not a public good. As we have explained, one feature of a pure public good is that it is impossible, or at best extremely costly, to charge people for using it. That aspect of television was changed when a practical means was devised for "scrambling" the signal sent out and providing a way for the viewer (at a cost) to unscramble it within his own set.[1] Subscribers are given or rented the necessary attachment. Payments are made either on a monthly basis or by means of a coin-operated switch mechanism on the descrambler box. It is obvious that pay TV needs no commercials because it is paid for directly by the consumer. That is, it is not a public good.

However, there are certain common-property aspects shared by both free and pay TV, as well as by radio. In the early days of commercial radio, anybody who wanted to could transmit; nobody owned any particular frequency and all were common property. Soon, though, one man's signal began interfering with another's. The solution chosen

[1] Pay TV was first envisioned by Matty Fox of Universal Pictures, Inc. He entered into a royalty agreement for rights to a scrambler-signal punch-card air system developed by Skiatron Electronics and Television Corporation of New York.

by the government was to license the use of each frequency on a noneconomic basis; that is, people could not directly bid for frequencies in an open market. If you did not have a license you would have been arrested for transmitting over commercial wavelenghts. Since only a limited number of licenses were issued, their owners enjoyed a monopoly reflected in the value of the license.[2]

TV-station licenses were later issued on a similar basis, and recipients were treated to immediate increases in the value of their company's stock. Although the licenses can be bought and sold, a present-day buyer will not capture the monopoly benefit because the owner will not sell his license at anything less than its total (discounted) monopoly value. The only alternative for a would-be entrant into the field is to attempt to get the FCC to take away the license of an existing station and reassign it without requiring the payment of its market value. Under such conditions, and since TV licenses are scarce and valuable commodities, it is not surprising that outsiders (nonowners of licenses) have frequently tried to gain control of functioning stations by legal challenges.

[2] *Monopoly rents.*

THE ECONOMICS
OF FLOODING
HELL'S CANYON

Hell's Canyon, on the Snake River separating Oregon from Idaho, is the deepest canyon on the North American continent, exceeding even the Grand Canyon. It offers some of the most spectacular scenery in the country; it is a natural habitat for elk, deer, and bighorn sheep; the hillsides echo to the call of vast flocks of redleg partridge; and the rushing river contains salmon, steelhead, and sturgeon.

Hell's Canyon is also perhaps the best remaining site in the United States for developing hydroelectric power. The results of such a development would be a high dam which would turn the river into a huge lake, backing it all the way up to an already existing dam and lake further up the river.

Should this new dam be built?

The issue created a controversy that has continued for many years. During this time the plans and proposed sites for the dam have changed. The protagonists on either side have also changed (in some cases they have even changed sides). And what was once a controversy between public and private power over two alternative and mutually exclusive dam sites has become a debate between those who want no dam at all and the now-unified forces of the public and private power groups who contend that the dam should be constructed and operated by their joint efforts.

While rhetoric and power politics have dominated the headlines, the issue has been fought before the Federal Power Commission with numbers. The numbers have been plugged into benefit–cost analyses of the dam; and, since several alternative dam combinations have been proposed, alternative benefit–cost analyses have been developed. We shall look at just one—the High Mountain Sheep Dam, clearly the most impressive hydroelectric proposal.

Benefit–cost analysis has been developed to help determine the social as distinguished from the private profitability of economic activities. What's the difference? For the production of a vast array of goods and services there is either no difference, or one so little that no one bothers about it. In such cases, the private opportunity costs of the amount of capital and the expected returns dictate whether to undertake an economic activity. For instance, if a predicted rate of return exceeds the opportunity cost of capital for a proposed factory, the factory will be built.

However, where externalities exist—that is, where benefits or costs accrue to persons other than the investor (and the user)—the purely private calculation may yield the wrong decision from the viewpoint of society as a whole. In the case of the High Mountain Sheep Dam project, a private investor undertaking the project would not get the benefits of the additional power that could be generated at downstream power plants as a result of regulating the flow of the river and releasing more water at periods of low-stream flow. Nor would a private investor reap the benefits from reducing flood damage in the lower Snake and Columbia rivers as a result of reducing stream flow in periods of high water and potential flooding. On the other hand, neither would that investor bear the costs to society of destroying or damaging the runs of migratory fish; reducing wildlife habitat, both waterfowl and mammal; and irrevocably altering the scenic beauty of a unique and irreplaceable area.

Some of these externalities are relatively easy to measure.

One is the downstream benefits of a dam, which are simply the value of the additional power generated times the price per kilowatt/hour. Another is the value of reduced flood damage, which can be calculated by assessing how much damage could be done downstream by the amount of water to be stored and multiplying that by the frequency with which such high water would occur in the absence of the dam (this data being obtainable from historical river records). But who can measure the externalities involved in the destruction of the aesthetic grandeur and recreational value of a previously undeveloped canyon? Let's see how this calculation was attempted in the case of High Mountain Sheep Dam.

Omitting, for the moment, the external costs associated with altering the environment, opponents of the dam measured all other costs and benefits of the proposed dam versus the next-best alternative, which was nuclear power. They then asked what value would have to be placed on preservation of the original environment to justify *not* building the dam.[1] The conclusion was that over its projected 50-year life span, the High Mountain Sheep Dam would provide benefits over its next-best alternative of between $14 and $24 million, depending on assumptions made about other dams and the nuclear alternative.

A brief resumé of the way the figures were derived will illustrate the usual procedure in such cases. The total investment cost of the dam with an interest rate of 9 percent was calculated at $266,786,000. That is, bonds would be floated at that interest rate to provide that sum. This brought the total annual costs (fixed charges on the bonds, plus costs for operating, generating, and transmission) to $39,597,000.

On the benefit side, the power benefits (presumably including downstream benefits) were $41,894,000 annually and the flood-control benefits were $245,000 annually, for a total of $42,139,000. Gross annual costs subtracted from gross annual benefits thus leave a net benefit of $2,542,000

[1] The following data are drawn from Dr. John Krutilla's testimony before the Federal Power Commision.

annually. This comes to $24,068,000 over the 50-year life-span of the project.

The last figure should bother you: A net annual benefit of $2.5 million multiplied by 50 years comes to a lot more than $24 million. Or does it? No, because a dollar earned to-day is considerably more valuable than a dollar earned next year, and about 75 times as valuable as a dollar earned 50 years hence. The reason for this is really quite simple. We must ask how many of today's dollars will be needed to make $2.5 million next year, recognizing that today's dollars can earn perhaps 9 percent (i.e., their opportunity cost and the rate at which we *discount* future dollars). A few simple calculations will convince you that the present value of $2.5 million 50 years from now (that is, the number of today's dollars needed to provide $2.5 million at 9 percent annual compound interest) is not that great. So the further away the benefit in time and the higher the opportunity cost of money (the interest rate), the lower the present value. The same reasoning applies to costs. When all the arithmetic is worked out, $24 million appears as the upper-bound estimate. The lower-bound estimate of $14 million was calculated in similar fashion using a different interest (discount) rate.

Now we come to the critical question. Is the value of preserving the existing canyon equal to $14–24 million over the next 50 years? How do you measure the enjoyment of a natural scenic attraction? The ideal answer would be ob-tained by assessing what people would be willing to pay to maintain the canyon. We have no answer, but we can get a little closer by some indirect methods. We find that in Nor-way, for example, where streams can be owned privately, sports fishermen are willing to pay as much as $500 a day for fishing rights in certain Atlantic salmon stream areas. Since the steelhead is a close cousin of the Atlantic salmon, we can get some notion of the value people place upon such fishing in the Hell's Canyon. Canadian Atlantic salmon leas-ing prices give further information. We can also attempt to discover how willing people have been to pay for hunting and other forms of recreation under market conditions by similar means.

Furthermore, it is clear that the value of recreational resources is growing each year, as increased income and leisure time enable more and more people to enjoy such facilities. Since the demand is increasing at all prices but the supply is fixed,[2] the value will inevitably keep rising. Overall, by such approximations, the authors of the rebuttal study for High Mountain Sheep Dam concluded that the recreational benefits of the original canyon do indeed surpass the $14–24 million of benefits to be expected from hydroelectric development.

We have presented the data for the opponents. The issue is not yet resolved and we shall have to await further evidence. But the economic methods and techniques are there, even if the necessary information is still inadequate to enable the opposing sides to reach a consensus.

[2] Theoretically, substitutes do exist, but it is not clear how close they really are.

20

THE ECONOMICS
OF NONOWNERSHIP:
THE BRISTOL BAY SALMON FISHERY

It is time for another fairy tale. Imagine, if you will, a lush forest of towering pines and dense fir in some Never-Never-Land. No one owns it. However, since the time is the 1970s, and there is a demand for lumber, paper, and plywood, timbermen are now flocking to the area to take advantage of this free resource. The Prince who rules over the land in which this unenchanted forest is situated can see that soon all trees will disappear, for each lumberman wants to cut as much as he can to get as rich as he can, and no individual lumberman has any interest in protecting young trees or in reforestation. So, the Prince in his wisdom decrees:

1. Logging will begin at 6:00 a.m. June 15 and close October 1 at 6:00 p.m. in even-numbered townships and sections.
2. Logging will be permitted on Tuesdays and Fridays, subject to extension or restriction by field announcement.
3. A logging license to cost $25,000 must be purchased prior to April 1.
4. It shall be unlawful for any person, firm, or corporation to use, employ, or operate a power-driven saw for the purpose of removing timber.

5. Hand axes must have a blade less than four inches but more than three inches with a handle to exceed eighteen inches. No logger shall have in his possession more than one axe.

6. Each axe shall be legibly marked with the registration number and initials of the operator. No axe shall be placed or operated less than 600 feet from any other axe.

7. No logging truck shall be longer than 30 feet overall, except trucks that logged prior to January 1, 1960.

8. Trees with cones can be taken only prior to July 31.[1]

Now that is an unlikely tale[2] because forests are owned by private individuals or companies or by a government. The oceans of the world, however, and even the inland waters are not owned, and the result is a fantasy world of irrational restrictions. The distinction between "owned" and "not owned" property is crucial to understanding the incentives that govern the use of resources. Let us examine in detail one such case.

Bristol Bay in central Alaska is the home of one of the richest runs of sockeye salmon in the world. The sockeye, or red salmon, is the most valuable of the existing five species of salmon. The return of spawning fish to Bristol Bay each summer attracts American commercial fishermen in ever-increasing numbers, while at the same time Japanese fleets are fishing for the catch outside the Alaskan territorial limits. In 1900, 8.5 million fish were taken from Bristol Bay; by 1917, the yearly catch had increased to 24.5 million. The salmon run declined alarmingly after World War II, however. In an attempt to reverse the trend, regulations over the season, fishing hours, boats, and gear increased in com-

---

[1] The preceding "regulations" are excerpted from Donald E. Bevan, "Methods of Fishery Regulation," in J. A. Crutchfield (ed.), *The Fisheries: Problems in Resource Management* (Seattle: University of Washington Press, 1965) pp. 25–40.

[2] However, it would not have been impossible in feudal times. Much land was then held in common, and the population growth of the twelfth and thirteenth centuries caused a similar pattern of exploitation. The consequences in Western Europe were the gradual development of property rights to land.

plexity until they paralleled in almost every detail the fantastic edicts handed down by our imaginary Prince.

BRISTOL BAY SALMON FISHING REGULATIONS[3]

1. *Fishing Seasons:* January 1–December 31.
2. *Weekly Fishing Periods:* Generally 9:00 a.m. Monday to 9:00 a.m. Saturday.
3. *Gear:* Drift gill nets in most districts. Trolling allowed in all waters.
4. *Gill-Net Specifications:*
   (a) Gill-net mesh not less than 5⅜ inches.
   (b) Gill nets not more than 28 meshes in depth.
   (c) Max. aggregate of drift of gill nets shall not be more than 150 fathoms in length.
   (d) Vessel registered may not have aboard more than legal limit of drift gear in aggregate.
   (e) Max. aggregate length, set gill nets not more than 50 fathoms in length.
   (f) Individual allowed two set gill nets.
   (g) Operation of set gill net only by fisherman in whose name it is registered.
   (h) Set gill nets shall be operated in straight line.
   (i) Fishing w/set gill nets limited to beach areas that at mean low water are connected by and exposed to shore. Inshore end of net above mean low water.
   (j) etc.—registration regulations.
5. *Identification of Gear:*
   (a) Bright red flag or buoy at each end of drift gill net, marked w/ registration number.
   (b) Marker on set gill net above high tide inshore of net.
   (c) [etc.]
6. *Minimum Distance Between Units of Gear:*
   (a) Set gill nets—300 ft. apart.
   (b) Drift gill nets—300 ft. apart.

[3] Summary—many exceptions for certain areas. Taken from the *State of Alaska Administrative Code,* Title 5, Chapter 6 (Bristol Bay Area), Article 3 (5AAC 06.310–5AAC 06.370).

7. *Vessel Specifications & Operation & Identification:*
   (a) No vessel over 32 ft. long.
   (b) Display registration number in symbols at least 12 inches high.
8. *Closed Waters:* About five areas in Nushagak Bay; two in Kulchak Bay, and several others.
9. *Registration:*
   (a) Must register for specific district.
   (b) Cannot change to another district before 48 hours after re-registration.
   (c) Cannot change gear before 48 hours after re-registration.
   (d) No gear or vessel eligible for fishing during 48-hour waiting period.
   (e) [Rest of section is hours and locations, and notification of local representatives.]

Naturally, the results in real life are more like a nightmare than a fairy tale. Fishermen are poor because they are forced to use inefficient equipment and to fish only a small fraction of the time, and of course there are far too many of them. The consumer pays a much higher price for red salmon than would be necessary if efficient methods were used. Despite the ever-growing intertwining bonds of regulations, the preservation of the salmon run is still not assured.

The root of the problem lies in the current nonownership arrangement. It is not in the interests of any individual fisherman to concern himself with perpetuation of the salmon run. Quite the contrary: It is rather in his interests to catch as many fish as he can during any one season.

Contrast this with a hypothetical world in which Bristol Bay would be private property. The owner would have a dual incentive: to use the most efficient technology to catch salmon at least cost, and to permit enough to escape to perpetuate the runs.

Two alternatives are open to a government for the regulation of a common-property resource: (a) restriction on efficiency but not on entry into the industry, which produces the horrendous results described above; (b) restriction on entry, but not on efficiency. This can be accomplished, for example, by an auction system where the highest bidders obtain rights to a limited number of fish. This is an "efficient" solution (in economic terms) but is subject to some drawbacks relative to distribution of income. The highest bidders would tend to be groups with enough capital to buy the best equipment. They could, therefore, outbid other, perhaps poorer groups. In underdeveloped areas, these could include fishermen from the indigenous population. The probability should also be considered that, via the political process, certain already favored groups would continue to receive benefits in the allocation of fishing rights, through such techniques as preferential tax legislation or government subsidy.

These, however, are merely "undesirable" distributional aspects, and should not be confused with the overall efficiency aspects of changing common property (oceans) to private property.[4]

Notice that, until recently, it would have been immeasurably difficult, or even impossible, to maintain and enforce private rights in the ocean, but the invention of modern electronic sensing equipment has now made the policing of large bodies of water relatively cheap and easy. Through the centuries it has often become feasible for common property to give way to private property precisely because technology has made possible the enforcement of private rights (exclusivity).

We are not saying that making the oceans into private property is "good." We are saying that doing so would lead to more output and fewer ecological disasters, although very probably at the risk of real problems relative to the distribution of gains and losses.

---

[4] Moving from an inefficient to an efficient economic situation always, by definition, increases output. Out of the increases "injured" parties can be compensated. In the case of native fishermen, their income might be maintained at least at the level they could have achieved by their own methods of fishing.

21

THE ECONOMICS
OF THOMAS MALTHUS
AND HIS PRESENT-DAY FOLLOWERS

Earlier in this book we examined the economics of population size. We saw that historically during some periods, population has grown faster than food supplies, and that the results have been recurring eras of famine or disease decimating a population weakened by undernourishment.

In the Western world, Thomas Malthus' dire predictions about the tendency for population to outrun the food supply were being undermined at the very time he was writing (at the end of the eighteenth century) as a result of widespread increases in productivity in both agricultural and nonagricultural areas. Before we turn to the present-day prophets of doom, it will be useful to look at the economics of Malthus' argument and to examine how it has been affected by increases in productivity.

Malthus was writing just at the time when the British population was experiencing an unprecedented growth. The result was that the demand for foodstuffs at all prices was increasing at a dramatic rate. In the short run this shift of the demand schedule coupled with a fixed, positively sloped supply schedule led to soaring food prices. However, the longer-run consequences was that farmers put more land into cultivation, the supply at all prices increased, and prices fell.

As population continued to grow, the farmers in England eventually used up all the good land and additional food had to be grown on poorer land or by applying more labor and capital (tools and equipment) to existing land. That is, increasing amounts of labor and capital were required to produce an additional unit of food output. The result was an increase in food output only at a higher cost. The factor of production, land—which is relatively fixed in supply— had thus caused *diminishing marginal returns* and the dismal predictions of Malthus' model followed.

What later upset his prediction was a change in productivity; that is, men became able to produce more output with the same inputs of labor, capital, and land because the quality of these inputs improved. Because of greater knowledge, improved seed, more efficient machinery (capital), etc., men were able to get more food from a given area of land at no extra costs, or indeed, at even lower cost. Moreover, by Malthus' time another alternative had become available. A man could produce manufactured goods and trade them with producers in those parts of the world where land was still abundant (such as America), thereby avoiding the consequences of diminishing returns in agriculture at home. The English did both. Malthus' predictions were confounded.

But that was in an era when the world's population was less than 1 billion and vast empty areas still existed. Today, population approaches 4 billion and could amount to considerably more by the end of the century. Few virgin lands are left, and their innate fertility is, with exceptions, not likely to be high. But it is not only man's sheer numbers that give an accurate guide to the rate at which he is gobbling up resources in advanced countries; it is also the income and rate of consumption of each man (relative to his ancestors or to people in poorer countries). For example, in 1960 in the United States, the per capita consumption of crude oil was 700 gallons (for automobiles and heating);

bituminous coal was 4,000 pounds (converted to electricity or used as an input in manufacturing; steel was 1,100 pounds; salt was 300 (only a small fraction of which was for seasoning); etc.

It is not surprising that a new generation of Malthusians has emerged to warn us that we are headed toward mass famine or, at the very least, toward the end of an era of spendthrift abundance. After all, the size of the earth is limited, so we do have a fixed factor. Sooner or later we will have dug up all the minerals, siphoned off all the oil, and stretched the capacity of agricultural lands until the food supply can increase no more, or can do so only at the expense of using a prohibitively greater percentage of our labor and capital.

That may be the ultimate fate of mankind, but there is no evidence that it is happening yet. In fact, quite the contrary. Productivity is increasing in extractive industry (agriculture, mining, forestry) so that, with a few exceptions (in forestry, for the most part), we are getting greater output with *less* input of labor and capital.

American agriculture faces surpluses, not shortages. At the time of the American Revolution approximately 90 percent of Americans worked in agriculture. By 1929 the figure was 22 percent, and at the present time it is less than 5 percent and still falling. It is not just the percentage of people in agriculture that is decreasing; the absolute number in agriculture is also on the decline. In 1910 the farm population consisted of 32.1 million people. By 1967 it had fallen to 11 million. In 1820 each farm worker produced enough food and fiber to support four persons. Today he supplies forty persons. In addition, the amount of land in agriculture has fallen absolutely from 365 million acres in 1929 to 308 million acres in 1967. During this same period, the total of crops raised on this land increased 50 percent and livestock (and livestock products) increased by 86 percent. In short, despite an absolute decline in farmland and labor, agriculture is producing vastly more than it did in earlier times.

But we don't need to rely on these general figures. Detailed studies of the production of individual agricultural, mining, and forest products usually show declining labor costs per unit of output between 1910 and 1960.[1] In effect we are moving in the reverse direction from that predicted by later-day Malthusians.

What is the explanation for this situation? Partly, it exists because the amount of nonrenewable resources in the earth is staggering in magnitude. In the case of minerals, for example, one reputable expert has estimated that if the earth's crust were a perfectly homogeneous mass with minerals distributed uniformly, each cubic mile of rock would hold a billion tons of aluminum, 625 million tons of iron, and so forth down to the relatively scarce minerals—650,000 tons of copper, 185,000 tons of lead, and 60 tons of gold. However, since minerals are more concentrated, the amount of the earth's surface already mined is still a miniscule fraction of the potential. A second explanation is that when diminishing marginal returns have set in for a resource, the resultant rise in price has tended to encourage a search for substitutes to replace it. But the overwhelming reason (which stems in part from the second explanation) is that technological advances have occurred at such a rate that increases of supply at all prices have outrun the parallel outward move in the demand schedule. There are undoubtedly other costs, not included here, which are by-products of this exploitation of resources; but for the United States, the plain simple fact is that we are not running out of resources, as that term is usually conceived.

But what about the rest of the world? No one can doubt that population in Egypt, India, China, and some other parts of the world has increased at a startling rate, and that agricultural productivity has not appeared to be keeping up. But that situation may be changing. The United States in its formulative years experienced a substantial lag between the systematic development of research and a payoff in improved agricultural productivity. We have only recently begun comparable research activity in other foodstuffs that are the staples for the non-Western world, but we are al-

[1] These studies are to be found in H. Barnett and C. Morse, *Scarcity and Growth* (Baltimore: Johns Hopkins Press, 1963), ch. viii.

ready beginning to get results that equal the dramatic productivity increases of American agriculture. The development of new strains of rice, wheat, maize, and soybeans are already resulting in output increases which appear to parallel the American experience of the past 40 years. Tiny Japan with its crowded acreage is already self-sufficient in rice production, while India, a wheat importer since the late nineteenth century, now appears self-sufficient in that basic cereal.

However, we should be cautious at this point. The long-run success of man's efforts entails more than enormous increases in the productivity of agriculture. On the other side of the ledger a decline in population fertility rates is necessary to provide any comfortable assurance of long-run success. No one can guarantee in perpetuity a sustained productivity increase in agriculture such as the United States has experienced in the past 40 years. But the present technological improvements do provide *at least* breathing space during which man can choose to reduce fertility rates throughout the world.

22

THE ECONOMICS
OF CRIME PREVENTION

In 1969, the Seattle City Council voted to permit 21 murders, 104 rapes, 962 robberies, and 417 assaults, as well as various numbers of lesser crimes, in the first half of 1970.

Stated in other terms, the Seattle City Council voted $17,916,986 for the police department that year. We (and the City Council) start our examination with an assumption that the amount of resources devoted to crime prevention is inversely correlated to the amount of crime. Had the City Council voted twice that amount, there would have been less crime. But how much less? In short, what is the relation between prevention of crime and money spent? How did the Council decide on that figure?

Before we can begin to answer these questions, we must look in greater detail at the economics of fighting crime. First of all, it is not only the police and other law-enforcement agencies that are used in crime prevention. The courts and various types of penal and reform institutions also enter the project, as do such devices as burglar alarms, locks, and safes. In total, more than $21 billion was spent to combat crime in the United States in 1965 (4 percent of net national product).

Like any other area of complex modern living, criminal-law enforcement has many aspects and the costs of each must be considered in allocating the resources available. First is the detection of a crime (in such cases as narcotics or prostitution) and the arrest of suspects. Next, costs are involved in the trial and conviction of the prisoner; they depend on the efficiency and speed with which the law-enforcement officials and the courts can act. Third, once the sentence is imposed, we are faced with the economic costs of maintaining and staffing prisons. But more important are the social implications of the question: What sorts and durations of punishment are most effective as deterrents to crime? Let's examine, from an economic standpoint, each of the phases of law enforcement.

The amount of resources devoted to discovering and apprehending criminals is obviously directly related to a reduction in crime. But the optimum allocation of those resources is not so clear-cut. The Chief of Police or the Commissioner is faced by two sets of problems. On the one hand, he must decide how to divide the funds between capital and labor— that is, shall he choose more cars, equipment, and laboratories; or more policemen, detectives, and technicians? On the other hand, he must also allocate his funds among the various police details within the department; for example, he could decide whether to clamp down harder on homicide or on car theft.

Within a law-enforcement budget of a given size he must, then, determine the optimum combination of production factors. The ideal combination is one in which an additional dollar spent on any one of the labor or capital inputs will provide an equal additional amount of enforcement. If an additional dollar spent on laboratory equipment yields a higher crime-deterrent result than the same dollar spent on a policeman's salary, the laboratory will win. While it is clear that inputs cannot be measured in such small amounts, the question of *indivisibility*[1] does not alter the basic argument. Nor does it alter the argument to recognize that we cannot precisely measure the returns on an increase in labor or in some input of capital. The police captain must normally judge from experience and intuition, as well as from available data, whether buying more cars or hiring more men will do the better job in checking crime. And note that his decision may change with changes in relative price. For example, when the salaries of policemen are raised, the balance may tip toward the use of more cars or equipment, depending on how well capital can be substituted for labor in a given situation. Instead of using two patrolmen in a car it might be economically efficient to equip the car with bulletproof glass and let the driver patrol alone.

The second task of the police chief is to determine how to allocate his resources among the interdepartmental details. Sometimes highly publicized events may influence his decision. For example, in 1969, prostitution increased in downtown Seattle to such a degree that local merchants protested vigorously that streetwalkers were hurting business. They had sufficient political influence to induce the police chief to sharply step up the detection and apprehension of prostitutes. That meant using more men and equipment on the vice squad; and within the restriction of a fixed budget this could be done only by pulling them from homicide, robbery, and other details which were thus made shorthanded. In effect, the cost of reducing prostitution was a short-run increase in assault and robbery. It is not clear (in the short run, at least) that political pressure of the sort just mentioned leads to a concentration of police enforcement in those areas that many people feel are most essential.

We said that three general areas of law enforcement entail costs to society, and have just dealt with the area of detection and arrest. The second area is trial and its outcome.

[1] A good or service is said to be indivisible if it can be sold only in relatively large quantities. For example, one cannot purchase one-tenth of a police car. However, perhaps the car can be rented for one-tenth of each month. Given the possibility of rental, many products can no longer be called indivisible.

Recent studies indicate that the likelihood of conviction is a highly important factor (if not the major one) in the prevention of crime. Currently, the probability of conviction and punishment for crime is extremely low in the United States. In New York City, it is estimated that a man who commits a felony faces less than one chance in two hundred of going to jail.[2] Lack of detection is one part of the explanation for this incredible figure; court congestion is another. In highly urbanized environments, the court calendar is so clogged that the delay in getting a case to trial may stretch from months into years.[3] One consequence of this situation is an increasing tendency for the prosecuter and suspect to arrange a pretrial settlement rather than further overburden the courts. This is what happens to 80 to 90 percent of criminal charges. The effect on the morale of the policemen who have brought the cases to trial is painfully obvious. Society may be underinvesting in the resources necessary to improve this process. If more were heavily spent on streamlining court proceedings instead of concentrating so heavily on making arrests, cases could be brought to trial more promptly, the presence of all witnesses could be more easily secured, and the hand of the D.A. would not be forced in making "deals" with suspects. Faced with the probability of quick and efficient trial, a potential criminal might think harder about robbing a bank or mugging a pedestrian. Chief Justice Burger himself has recently declared that we do in fact need an overhauling of our courts.

There remains another issue which is highly controversial. The likelihood of detection and conviction can be increased by new technical means, wiretapping, and by changes in the laws protecting the rights of suspects (e.g., by permitting law officers to enter and search without knocking, lifting the requirement that suspects be informed of their Constitutional rights, and allowing the holding of suspects incommunicado for lengthy periods). However, the costs of such

[2] *Wall Street Journal* (August 20,1970).
[3] Many court calendars are solidly booked for 2, 3, or even 5 years into the future. In New York, for example, the average time lapse between filing a civil suit and getting it to trial is 39 months.

legal changes in terms of infringement on individual liber-
ties are extremely serious, and in any event we do not have
the information necessary to determine how effective such
changes would be.

We come now to the third area of law enforcement,
the effectiveness of prison sentences as a deterrent to crime.
Data taken from various states show that after the influence
of other factors has been taken into account, severe prison
sentences do indeed reduce certain types of criminal activity, but have no apparent effect on others. Longer terms
have proved effective in cutting down crimes against property (which suggests a benefit–cost calculation on the part of
potential thieves). But the length of sentences seemed less
significant in deterring crimes against persons (murder, rape,
assault) and appeared to have no bearing in the case of un-
premeditated murder.

We can now return to our original question. How did the
Seattle City Council determine that a budget for crime prevention of $17,916,868 for 1969 was the right amount? In
the short run, they were faced with a total budget of a given
size and had to decide how to carve it up between law enforcement and other municipal demands, such as fire protection, health, parks, streets, and libraries. Just as a Police
Chief can try to determine what combination of men and
equipment within his fixed budget will deter the greatest
amount of crime, a City Council will attempt to choose a
combination of spending on all agencies that will yield the
maximum amount of public services. If additional money
spent on fire protection does not yield as much "good" as
it would if spent on police protection, then the amount
should be allocated to law enforcement.[4] Determining the
value of services rendered by each agency of course poses
a touchy problem. However, it is not insuperable, at least in
principle. We saw in the case of the Hell's Canyon issue
(Chapter 19) that crude approximations can be made of
the benefits and costs of recreation. This can be applied
equally to other nonpriced goods and services, and the

[4] The City Council equates on the margin returns from money spent on
all municipal activities.

efficiency of the public sector of our economy will be improved as such calculations are made and refined.

The short-run constraint of a fixed budget for law enforcement may be altered in the long run by going to the state legislature and asking for increased funds for crime prevention. The legislature then has to wrestle with the same allocation problem that has engaged the City Council. Funds can be increased for a city's budget only by tightening the belt in some other area such as school expenditures or park development. The same, now-familiar calculations must now be made on the state level: Will spending an additional dollar on higher education yield greater returns for society than the same dollar given to a City Council to allocate to crime prevention? The same difficult problem arises in measuring the dollar value of nonpriced services resulting from any given state expenditure.

The state does have an option not open to the City Council in most states. It can raise taxes. Now we have widened the allocation problem. The increased taxes will reduce the disposable income of some part of the citizenry. Those who pay the additional taxes must in turn decide whether they feel the additional public services made available are worthwhile. For example, they must decide whether the reduction in crime attributable to an increased expenditure on law enforcement is as valuable to them as the goods they could have enjoyed from that increased tax money. If they do not think so, then at the next election they will vote to "throw the rascals out."

The above description indicates that nonmarket solutions to economic problems run basically parallel to market solutions. Although we have focused on crime prevention, the issues are similar for all types of government decisions and for all levels of government—local, state, and federal.

But certain differences must also be noted between decision-making in the private market sector of the economy and in the public nonmarket sector. Problems of measurement are much greater in the latter. How do we put a price tag on recreation, which is the output of the Parks Department? For another thing, the signals come through much louder and more clearly in market situations in which changes in private profitability "telegraph" to entrepreneurs what policies will be best.[5] Instead of market signals, the maker of public policy receives a confused set of noises generated by opponents and proponents of his decisions. A legislator is in the unenviable position of trying to please as many of the electorate as possible while operating with very incomplete information.

Concerning crime prevention, we can suggest one way in which the allocation of resources might be altered in a perhaps more economically efficient direction. Right now in almost all cities and states in the Union, a man beaten up in the streets and left with permanent brain damage has no one to sue for his injuries. If the attacker is caught he will be jailed. That really does not help the victim, who actually ends up paying part of his taxes for the prisoner's room and board!

If, on the other hand, the city or state were held liable for all damages sustained, the victim (or his dependents) could sue the city or state for compensation. Unlimited liability on the part of government for crimes against the populace would certainly alter the present allocation of resources between crime prevention and other public endeavors. Under present laws the private cost of crime is borne by the individual and he has little hope of being compensated. It is true that five states now provide some liability, but it is certainly not enough.[6] Right now, no state has to pay the full cost of crime against the public. Hence suboptimal expenditures for crime prevention and control now prevail.

Crime costs. So does crime prevention. But the latter also has benefits to society which can be weighed in the making of decisions about law-enforcement methods and expenditures.

[5] In instances where externalities exist, it may be to society's advantage to alter these signals by appropriate measures.
[6] New York, California, Hawaii, Maryland, and Massachusetts have paid out $1.8 million to 1,000 crime victims, or $1,800 per crime.

23

THE ECONOMICS OF INDENTURED
SERVANTS AND OTHER FORMS
OF HUMAN-CAPITAL INVESTMENT

We forswore slavery in 1863 and indenture of human beings even earlier. The former was a type of involuntary servitude with bitter consequences. The latter was, for the most part,[1] a voluntary agreement. In return for ship passage from the Old World to the New, and for some payment at termination, the indentured servant pledged himself to work for a period of 5 to 7 years. The individual who provided passage money also offered perquisites at the conclusion of the indenture in the form of two suits of clothes, two hoes, one axe, and perhaps a mule and some land. Indentured servants were a major source of labor in the American colonies, and thousands of our forefathers (and mothers) migrated to the New World by such an arrangement. This form of servitude was based upon a legally recognized property right which extended for the period of indenture. The investor had assurance that his investment in passage money would pay off because the servant could not legally renege on his employment. In effect, the investor had a legally recognized

[1] There was some involuntary indenture of felons.

property right in a fellow human being for a limited period of time.

As noted before, a major role of the capital market is to supply businessmen with money to build plants and buy machinery. The businessman plans to use the borrowed money in such a manner as to earn enough to pay back the lender and still make a profit. Some loans are unsecured;[2] that is, they do not use physical plant or equipment as collateral but rather rely on the good credit reputation of the company. Such loans accordingly are more risky and involve a higher interest rate than loans secured by real collateral. More typical, however, is the borrower who pledges plant or equipment as collateral for the loan so that, in case his business venture does not succeed, the creditor has some tangible assets to receive in either partial or full payment for the defaulted loan. The better the collateral the lower the risk and, accordingly, the lower the interest rate charged for the loan.

What is the difference between borrowing money to invest in plant and equipment with the expectation of realizing a profit, and investing in a human being with the same end in view? In the days of the indentured servant there was none, for in both cases the lender's investment was secured by collateral recognized by the law and recoverable in damages accordingly. That is no longer the case when one invests in other human beings. They are neither "property" nor "recoverable."

Yet in modern times we have come to recognize that investment in human beings contributes as much to economic growth as does investment in capital equipment. Because property rights are effective and enforced we do not need to worry about investment in new plant and equipment. The private profitability of such investment insures that interest rates will be "high" enough to attract suppliers of loanable funds into that market.[3] But what about the human-capital market? To operate our complicated technical equipment and the resulting complex organizational structure, we need

[2] Debentures are a good example.
[3] Assuming no problems of externality exist.

highly trained and educated engineers, scientists, and lawyers. If one form of capital is scarce relative to the other, the scarcer form normally commands a higher price. This situation will induce suppliers of loanable funds to invest in that form of capital. For example, if the interest rate on a loan to build a factory is 6 percent, but there is a dearth of skilled engineers to operate the factory, the price of engineers will rise. Accordingly, the rate of return on becoming an engineer (reflected in the present net value of his discounted earnings stream) will rise. In effect, the rate of return on investing in an engineer would rise to, say, 20 percent. Other things being equal, we would expect suppliers of funds to shift from the physical-captial market to the human-capital market until the supply schedule of funds in the latter has increased so much that the quantity of engineers is sufficient to make the expected rate of return in both markets equal (an additional dollar invested in either market produces the same rate of return). But then, other things are *not* equal!

It is not that the rate of return on human-capital investment has not been high. Historically, it has paid to go to college; this payment is reflected in the lifetime-earnings stream of different educational levels. (See Chapter 24, "The Economics of Public Higher Education"). However, it is one thing for an entrepreneur to go to a bank, present his qualifications, and borrow money for a capital investment. It is something else when a student presents his academic credentials and asks to borrow the funds for a college education. The former can pledge the plant as collateral; the latter cannot offer equal security. Accordingly, bankers and other suppliers of funds have not been able to practice *arbitrage* (equating the rates of return by shifting funds from one market to another) in the market, since the security and risks cannot be equated because of the nature of property rights. The result has been a tendency in many countries to underinvest in human beings. This may have been the case historically in the United States.

24

THE ECONOMICS OF PUBLIC HIGHER EDUCATION

Since the market for human capital tends to be imperfect, it is thought that we have tended through the years to invest too little in that area, not spending enough on the education of our young. Historically that may have been true, but it is not clear that the assertion is tenable today. In fact, it is possible that we are currently investing too much.

Before taking a look at this possibility, suppose we first review what constitutes the "right" amount. The correct amount of higher education is one at which the social return on the investment in human capital is equal at the margin to other types of social investment (i.e., the opportunity costs of capital are equated at the margin). The social costs of higher education are (a) the direct costs—i.e., tuition, room, board, books; (b) an additional subsidy, in the case of public universities, which is provided by the state from tax revenues; and (c) the income forgone by the student while in college—i.e., his opportunity costs during the period he is a student. The social benefits are (a) the lifetime incremental earnings yielded the student by four years of college—i.e., the difference between the earnings he would have received during his lifetime as a high-school graduate and the earnings he will receive as a college graduate; (b) the consumption value of higher education—i.e., the value of an education for aesthetic enjoyment of books, art, music, etc.; (c) any external benefits that society receives from a better-educated citizenry. Both the costs and the benefits should be discounted back to the present to make them comparable. Calculations excluding the consumption return and possible external benefits have been made in various studies, and these show a rate of return of 10 to 15 percent.

There is no reason to expect that the opportunity costs of higher education will necessarily tend to be equated at the margin. To see why, let's look at colleges and universities from three different viewpoints—those of the student, of the parent, and of the state legislature. We will observe that each considers different parts of the total social costs and benefits in making the calculations.

The cost to the student is the income forgone during college plus whatever percentage of other college expenses he pays himself as distinguished from those paid by his parents. Children from poorer families tend to have to work their way through college and to shoulder a larger share of the direct costs. The benefits are the consumption benefits plus the increased lifetime-income stream. The lifetime earnings of a typical college graduate are about $185,000 more than those of a high-school graduate. The student pays only a portion, and usually a very small portion, of the costs, and receives all the consumption and investment benefits. It would clearly be worth his while to go to college, even if the social rate of return on college had fallen below the social equilibrium rate.

The parents, typically, bear the major share of the direct costs of a college education plus a part of the state subsidy as taxpayers. Costs approximate $2,000 per year for a state college for fees, books, room and board, etc. The benefits are vicarious. Parents enjoy watching the consumption and investment returns of their offspring and derive some prestige from boasting about their children graduating from college. Just what the equilibrium rate of investment for parents may be would be difficult to measure, but it is clearly not the same as for either students or legislators.

Legislators appropriate an amount of money each year to make up the difference between the tuition (plus any other income the university may receive) and the total costs of operating the university.[1] Grants from the federal government, endowments, foundations, and gifts provide additional funds. The rest of it must come from appropriations by the legislature. In the state of Washington, appropriations for all the institutions of higher learning (beyond the twelfth grade) for the 1968 biennium involved an expenditure by the state of approximately $400 million; this was 20 percent of the total budget and equal to $120 in tax monies for every man, woman, and child in the state.

Why do states subsidize higher education, and what determines the amount? Partly, they are influenced by parents of college students who form a potent political group and are receiving a subsidy from other taxpayers. Those who are subsidized obviously wish to perpetuate the system. Partly, the influence is the American heritage that education is a right (like free parks) that everyone should enjoy regardless of income. And partly it is that there is a widespread view that external benefits are associated with a more educated society.

The first contention is a matter of political survival and is hard to argue down, although it is probably the single most important cause of the continued high level of spending on higher education. The second contention implies that all who wish to do so should be able to go to college. This could become more of a reality if the market for human capital were perfected, perhaps by more government loans to students. The third contention may provide another clue to continued legislative support. It is widely contended that a better-educated society has less crime, less juvenile delinquency, etc., and that a higher proportion of college-

[1] For the University of Washington, as a more or less typical example, the tuition is $432 per person; totaled for all students this payment accounts for less than 10 percent of the university's budget.

educated adults in a state makes for a better society. How much truth this view contains is hard to say. Certainly, in recent years legislators have been shaken in their faith in a college education, and have come to perceive some external diseconomies to counter the alleged external economies.[2] Note, though, that such side effects are supposedly a function of *all* higher education, whether in the form of engineering training or liberal-arts training.

Most technical higher education involves very specific training, presumably useful to the student in a limited area of job pursuits. The technical student reaps the benefits (obtains a rate of return) from his specialized training. His employer has to pay him the value of his marginal product and so does not usually, in a competitive labor market, obtain excess returns from the skills of the specialized student. Therefore, it is not obvious that *government* should be subsidizing that part of schooling which is technical in nature.

The positive externalities—a more informed citizenry, less crime, etc.—appear historically to have come from *general* education, which requires fewer resources than does technical education. Unless it can be shown that technical education also generates positive externalities, there may be no valid argument for its subsidization.

[2] We should note that we have ignored two additional considerations which influence appropriations. The state legislature is concerned with benefits within the state—not with the general social welfare. This should tend to induce the legislator to raise out-of-state tuition, but it also means he cannot capture any benefits from graduates who move away. Moreover, the legislator may recognize another side benefit (externality) from a university which is probably of substantial magnitude—that is, achieves advances in knowledge from research. Again, however, most of the benefits from research redound to society as a whole, although some, such as agricultural research, may be specific to state problems and tend accordingly to be handsomely supported.

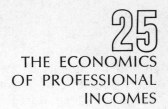

THE ECONOMICS
OF PROFESSIONAL
INCOMES

It is a well-known fact that professional people—doctors, dentists, lawyers, and some professors—make more than nonprofessionals. Are those who become professionals basically more able and smarter than the rest of society, or is there some other explanation for their high incomes? It appears that although innate ability and inherited wealth are important in determining the distribution of income, many other factors are also significant. Before we examine these, let us look at the statistics on professional incomes.

A 1954 study reported that on the average a professional worker earns between two and three times as much as a nonprofessional.[1] And an independent professional practitioner earns, on the average, four times as much as a nonprofessional salaried worker. Note, though, that independently earned incomes have much wider variations than do incomes for salaried workers. This fact fits in well with the

---

[1] Milton Friedman and Simon Kuznets, *Income from Independent Professional Practice* (New York: National Bureau of Economic Research, 1954).

empirical (and theoretical)[2] observation that the higher the risk (i.e., variation in attainable earnings) the larger the average incomes. This is true for all occupations and also for investments in nonhuman capital, such as common stocks. Further, the variation in income for the health profession exceeds that for legal services, accounting, and engineering. We will attempt to explain this last fact later on.

In trying to explain why some people earn more than others, or have more wealth than others, we must look at several considerations: (a) intelligence, (b) inherited wealth, (c) economic rents and individual tastes, (d) schooling, (e) productivity, (f) exploitation and discrimination, (g) monopoly, and (h) "good luck."

Points (a) and (b) are self-evident and need little explanation. One obviously has a better chance of earning more if he is born with more salable abilities, such as intelligence. Obviously one will be wealthier if he inherits a large estate, and indirectly this may also contribute to his ability to earn a large salary through better educational opportunities.

Point (c) needs more explanation. One who is a risk-preferer, if he is born handsome, or with a unique voice, or with exceptional guitar-playing abilities, may choose to try his luck in an occupation where the probability of success is extremely small but where those who succeed really cash in. The Beatles represent a good example. As an incipient rock group in Liverpool they made small incomes—much smaller than they could have made at that time as, say, truck drivers.[3] They opted for a low income with a small chance of eventually making a very large one. Once their specialized talents were discovered and promoted, they obtained that very large income. In fact, they obtained an income far exceeding what was needed to induce them to keep singing. Economists say that this "extra" income represents *economic rent* earned by their remarkably specialized resources.

[2] This is theoretically correct only when people are on the average risk-averse—i.e., have preferences against taking risks.
[3] We might view their Liverpool days as on-the-job training, which is a form of human-capital investment.

The same analysis holds for the Rolling Stones, Tom Jones, Frank Sinatra, Bob Dylan, Glenn Gould, Pablo Casals, Miles Davis, Jane Fonda, Peter Sellers, John Galbraith, Milton Friedman, Paul Samuelson, and Raquel Welch. They are all collecting economic rents—income over and above the amount that would induce them to continue in their present occupations.

Going on to point (d), we note that schooling is an investment in human capital; like any other investment it has associated costs, and it yields (hopefully) a stream of returns. The costs of schooling consist mainly of the forgone earnings the student could make during the time he is in school (opportunity cost of not working). The rate of return to the average college entrant for his investment in higher education is on the order of 10 to 15 percent per annum (the rate is even higher to male white urban college graduates); that is, their prospective income is higher than it would otherwise have been by that amount. The rate of return to investing in a high-school diploma appears to be higher than it is for a college degree, and the highest return is for investing in a grade-school education.

Professional people have to make the largest investment of all because of the additional cost of earnings forgone while in graduate or professional school. As would be expected, the anticipated income must be higher to induce people to forgo earnings (and hence consumption)[4] until they are in their middle or late twenties. (It should be noted that this latter statement does not necessarily hold with as much force for so-called "perpetual students.")

We should add here that cyclical variations occur in the returns to human-capital investment. The start of the 1970s is witnessing a cyclical downturn in the demand for Ph.D.s in academia, industry, and government. Hence people who started an investment in graduate chemistry four years ago are finding that the rate of return is lower than they had anticipated on the basis of historical evidence available at the time they began.

[4] If there were perfect competition, though, the discounted present value of income streams from all occupations would be equated on the margin.

Besides formal schooling, people also obtain the ability to increase their productivity and hence income (point e above) by on-the-job training (i.e., experience). We therefore expect income in any occupation to be positively correlated with age. And it is, up to about age 40 to 50. Thereafter it declines, partly because fewer hours are worked by people over 45. The specific age differs for different occupations and is obviously much lower for sex idols than for lawyers.

Exploitation and discrimination also affect the distribution of income (point f). Even with equal educational achievement (both in quality and quantity) certain groups may not, and actually do not, receive incomes equal to those of other groups. We will treat this important topic in the next chapter.

Next are the effects of monopoly power. If any group of sellers of a service or a product can create a monopoly, that group predictably will earn monopoly returns (rents) exceeding the amount it could otherwise have obtained. By viewing the American Medical Association as a form of monopoly one can explain much of its behavior and also the level of doctors' incomes.

Acting as monopolist, the AMA restricts the supply of licensed health personnel. As described before (p. 49 f.) this is done in several ways: by controlling entrance into medical schools and by keeping a tight rein over hospitals' ability to obtain interns, over doctors' access to hospitals for surgery, and so on. Note here that the individual doctors need not understand or knowingly participate in a monopoly pricing system for our analysis to be correct. It is only necessary that the leaders of the AMA act *as if* they understood.

Has the restriction of supply in medicine succeeded in making doctors' incomes higher than would be necessary to compensate them for their unusually long period of training? The evidence offered before suggests that this is the case. In addition, a study of 1959 income data revealed that incomes in the health industry (excluding hospital personnel) were remarkably bunched up at the very high end. That is to say, although the average income in the health industry was not necessarily higher than that of some other professions,[5] many more doctors were making very high incomes, even two to three times the average.[6]

The above evidence lends support to the assertion that the AMA acts as a monopoly, since this would explain the excess rents earned by doctors. Some recent studies, however, have provided evidence which challenges this notion.

The last factor which determines a person's income is chance or "good luck" (point h). This is one factor that cannot be developed by the individual. Indeed, if he waits for luck to bring his fortune, the odds are that he will end up in the lower part of the distribution of income.

---

[5] It was, compared to accounting and engineering.
[6] Victor R. Fuchs, E. Rand, and B. Garrett, "The Distribution of Earnings in Health and Other Industries," *The Journal of Human Resources*, Vol. V., No. 3 (Summer 1970), pp. 382–389.

26
THE ECONOMICS
OF EXPLOITATION
AND DISCRIMINATION

Urban nonwhite males earned approximately 40 percent less than urban white males in 1959.

Blacks obtain lower rates of return on the average from investing in a college education than do whites.

Ghetto dwellers pay more on the average for equal quality in housing, food, and clothing, than do nonghetto residents.

Do the above facts confirm that exploitation and discrimination exist? Before answering this question, we need to examine the economic connotations of these two explosive words.

The everyday meaning of exploitation is simply not being paid enough for what you sell (labor services or goods) and having to pay too much for what you buy. Discrimination is usually taken to mean about the same as exploitation, but may also include not being able to find work at all and not being able to buy a certain product, such as housing in particular neighborhoods.

The economist's definition of *exploitation* is somewhat more restrictive. We consider in this book that a person is being exploited in the selling of his labor services if he is being paid less than the value of his marginal product. He is being exploited in the buying of goods and services if he pays a price that exceeds the (marginal) cost of the product or service he is buying. (Note here that "cost" also includes normal profits.)

Using the above definition of exploitation, let's see how it is possible for this phenomenon to exist. First and foremost, lack of information allows exploitation. When employees are ignorant of better job opportunities, they may be exploited by employers. When consumers are unaware of other and cheaper product sources, they may be exploited by sellers.

Restricted entry is another cause of exploitation. When a professional sports league prevents the entry of competing leagues, players may be exploited because of the monopsony power of the single existing major league employer, as described in Chapter 12. If a food merchant in an isolated town successfully prevents entry by new firms, consumers can be forced to pay him monopoly rents over and above the competitive price of food.

Restricted mobility is another cause of exploitation. If a lawyer is prevented from practicing in states other than the one where he now works, he may be exploited because he is not allowed to go where the value of his services (and his potential income) is highest.[1]

It should be noted that each of the last three paragraphs included the phrase "may be exploited." Stress is placed on the "may." The lack of information, of free entry, and of mobility does not prima facie indicate exploitation. More is needed. In terms of information, all employees or consumers concerned must be unaware of the facts not—just the average employee or consumer. For example, non-English-speaking immigrants arriving in America could be exploited only when they first set foot on shore (and even then not for long) for there were brokers who specialized in providing them with translated information. Competition among immigrant brokers assured that non-English-speaking

[1] See letter to the Editor, *Ramparts* (August 1970).

employees received wages equal to the value of their marginal product.[2] The point here is that information need not be obtained directly by the employee himself, since competition among employers will provide sufficient information (at the margin) to insure nonexploitation. The same argument applies to the relation between consumers and sellers.

Nor is the mere lack of free entry enough to open the way for exploitation; those participating in the restricted side of the market must also agree among themselves not to compete against one another. Take, for example, the National Football League of 10 years ago. It restricted entry and *also,* via the "draft" system, prevented teams from bidding against each other. Otherwise, incentives for individual teams to compete for the best players normally would have netted players incomes equal to the value of their marginal products.

In general, then, exploitation requires restrictions on information, entry, and mobility plus additional arrangements to ensure that such restrictions affect *all* employees and consumers. Up to now we have been considering mainly the labor market. We now turn to product markets.

Ghetto consumers are known to pay higher prices for almost everything they buy. This is a true form of exploitation only if it can be demonstrated that the costs of providing products are no higher in ghettos than elsewhere. The evidence suggests that they are higher, because of: (a) relatively higher property insurance rates for ghetto businesses, (b) relatively higher "shrinkage" (theft) rates for ghetto stores, (c) relatively higher rates of violent crime in ghettos, and (d) relatively higher nonpayment for time purchases by ghetto residents.

It is true that the markup on ghetto-store products is higher than elsewhere, and that this tends to make for relatively higher net dollar profits on sales for ghetto merchants. But, after all the costs and taxes are taken out of these profits, the percentage rate of net return for ghetto retailers

[2] This was on average lower than for the native-born, because the ability to use English increased productivity.

on the money they have invested is lower than for general-market retailers.[3]

Exploitation as defined above may or may not exist in the ghetto; but there can be little doubt that *discrimination* does in fact exist or, as some economists euphemistically put it, that there are "tastes for discrimination" in our society.

We say that an employer has a taste for discrimination when he acts as if there were nonmoney costs associated with hiring blacks or other minority-group members. This behavior leads to lower incomes for blacks than they would receive otherwise.[4]

In a theoretical and empirical study of discrimination against blacks, Dr. G. S. Becker[5] found that discrimination: (a) is positively related to the relative numbers of blacks and whites, and further is more prevalent when large numbers are involved in nonmarket actions, such as the attainment of formal education; (b) is less for those seeking temporary as opposed to permanent work; (c) is greater for those who are older and better educated; and (d) has deterred some blacks considering entering a profession from trying to enter law because of their competitive disadvantage in arguing before white juries.

One of Dr. Becker's empirical conclusions was that "[black] incomes would increase by 16 percent if market discrimination ceased."[6]

Discrimination against blacks has in a very real sense prevented them from acquiring as much human capital as whites. Even if blacks attend school as long, their scholastic achievement is less, for they typically are allotted more meager school resources than their white counterparts. Data from the 1960 census revealed that a large portion of the

---

[3] Frederick D. Sturdivant (ed.), *The Ghetto Marketplace* (New York: The Free Press, 1969), p. 15.

[4] We defined exploitation as not receiving the value of one's marginal product. If we include the employer's psychic negative valuation of employing blacks, then discrimination does not imply exploitation; however, both result in lower incomes for those adversely affected.

[5] G. S. Becker, *The Economics of Discrimination* (Chicago: University of Chicago Press, 1957).

[6] *Ibid.*, p. 21.

white/nonwhite income differential results from differences in both the quantity of education received and scholastic achievement (which is a function *inter alia* of the quality of education received). "Differences between whites and nonwhites in these two education-related factors are estimated to have accounted for nonwhite urban males receiving between 23 and 27 percent less income than white urban males in 1959. The size of these estimates indicates that unless differences between the two populations in these two factors can be reduced substantially, the median income of nonwhite males is unlikely to increase to more than 70 to 80 percent of that of whites, *even if employment discrimination is substantially reduced* [emphasis added]."[7]

Black (and certain other minority groups) are suffering from, among other things, too small investment in their human capital. But even when we take account of differences in quantity of education received, scholastic achievement, and regional, age, and city-size distributions (all factors which affect productivity) there remains an unexplained differential in income between blacks and whites of 14 to 25 percent for nonfarm occupations.[8] We are left with the inevitable conclusion that this difference is due to discrimination.

[7] James Gwartney, "Discrimination and Income Differentials," *American Economic Review*, Vol. LX, No. 3 (June 1970), p. 397.
[8] *Ibid.*, p. 397.

27

THE ECONOMICS
OF DISTRIBUTING
FREE BREAD

Once upon a time there was a benevolent dictator who decided that no one in his country should be deprived of the basic necessities of life, so he decreed that henceforth bread would be free. Of course, the dictator expected that more poor people would get to eat bread after it became free. And for a little while the amount of bread consumed increased only modestly. But not for long. The quantity demanded at a zero price soon began to grow by leaps and bounds.

To meet this increased demand the dictator had many more bakeries built and had old ones expanded. Since his economy was already at full employment, the only way he could build and staff his bakeries was by withdrawing workmen and equipment from making shoes, houses, and other goods. The prices of these other goods went up accordingly, because their supply was reduced.

When the consumption of bread reached one hundred loaves a day for every man, woman, and child in his domain, the kindly dictator decided to find out where all the bread was going. He was at his neighborhood bakery the next morning when it opened. A man in overalls backed his truck up to the bakery and said, "Fill it up." He then took three more loaves of bread, put them in the cab of his truck and drove off. Following the man until he reached his farm, the ruler saw him take the three loaves into the kitchen and then feed the truckload of bread to his chickens.

The ending of the story is lost in the mists of time, but we do recall that the dictator was warmly beloved by the country's chicken farmers, who erected a statue in his honor.

The parable of free bread should be familiar, since earlier chapters have discussed the economic implications of free clams, free parks, free fishing, and even free medical care. But our primary interest in those chapters was the effect of a zero price on resource allocation. Here, we want to examine the effect upon income distribution.

If the price of a commodity is kept artificially high by monopolistic restrictions, then people will buy less of it than they would if competition were restored and the price were lower. Similarly, if the price is kept below the competitive equilibrium, people will buy more than they would at the competitive equilibrium price. How much less or more in each case depends upon the elasticity of demand for the product. In the case of clams, parks, and other such free goods, the demand is elastic enough so that it greatly exceeds the supply at a zero price. The result is the necessity of instituting some form of rationing. As noted in the chapter on clamming, this in effect makes people's subjective evaluation of queuing time very important. For it is on that basis that the decision is made whether to clam, to go to a park, etc. However, since richer people typically value their time more highly than do poorer people (since each group has a very different opportunity cost) the effect is to encourage relatively more use by lower-income groups.

The only way the government can eliminate rationing of "free" goods and still keep them "free" is to divert resources from other parts of the economy. But these diverted resources can then no longer be used by others. The additional free goods can no longer be called free.

When people talk of establishing free universal health

care they typically do not envision the possibility of unmeet-able demands. Rather, it is assumed that supply will always equal demand. Since the demand for health care appears to be quite price elastic, the amount demanded at a zero price will certainly exceed any quantity demanded at current prices. If universal medical care is to be supplied to all who wish it, an enormous diversion of resources from other sectors of the economy will be needed. Moreover, if we were to try to minimize the cost of the increased supply by establishing a ceiling on doctors' incomes, we would be producing precisely the results described in the case of the Pernambuco Tramway (see Chapter 5). Doctors would migrate elsewhere and students would take up other occupations, as has happened in Britain.

Granted that some solution must be found for the economic ills of a sector of our population. Is selective income distribution of the "free bread" variety really the answer? When free goods and services are established, the belief is being affirmed that we do not trust people to make the right judgment in spending their incomes.

And if the question comes up, "*What* income?" it might be pointed out that an alternative to free bread may be available in the form of some device for general income redistribution. One of these, the negative income tax proposal, is discussed in Chapter 30.

28

THE ECONOMICS
OF ECOLOGY
AND INCOME DISTRIBUTION

There are few more unsightly aspects to the urban environment than the jungle of poles and overhead wires that foul the typical cityscape. When we extend the term pollution to include visual pollution, overhead wires are a prime candidate for inclusion in this category. The solution is to place them underground, and this process is going on in many cities around the United States.

Typically, the relocating of arterial wiring is paid for by a general rate increase; but in residential areas, it is not uncommon for the citizens of an area who want this change to form an L.I.D. (Local Improvement District), develop a plan, and submit it to the appropriate body for approval. Usually the utility company pays part of the cost and each lot owner pays a proportionate share of the rest (in Seattle, the ratio has been approximately 50–50). Placing wires underground in an already developed residential area is expensive, with the total amounting to as much as $1,800 per lot. It is not surprising that this type of cost-sharing has tended to restrict most underground wiring to higher-income areas. However, since the share paid for by the utility company comes from the general income received from everyone's rates, while benefits accrue to the upper-income groups, such projects reflect a redistribution of income from poor to rich.

Two alternative options exist. We could insist that the lot owner pay the entire cost of placing wiring underground, in which case there would be no redistribution but also, probably, very little change. Or, we could let the utility company raise rates sufficiently to alter the wiring of the whole city, in which case everyone would pay. At a recent public hearing on the subject in Seattle, the head of the local utility company testified that such a program stretching over a 10-year period would necessitate a doubling of electric rates. A rate increase bears more heavily on the poor because the percentage of their income that goes for electricity is typically greater than the percentage for the rich. Thus the consequence is again to impose a greater relative burden on the poor than the rich. Is the case of underground wiring different in its effects on income distribution from other solutions to environmental problems?

Before we attempt to answer this thorny question, we reiterate here a fact of which all readers should now be well aware. Every action has a cost. That is, every action involves some opportunity cost, whether or not this cost is explicitly stated or even understood by those incurring it. Since our world is one of limited resources, it is also a world of trade-offs. In the underground-wiring example, we can trade off higher electric rates (or smaller amounts of income to spend on other things) for beauty (no overhead wires). Beauty does not come to us free of charge. When it is realized that every alternative course of action involves certain sets of costs, then it is time to ask, "Who will bear these costs?" We have already seen what happened in one case. We can now discuss others.

Many citizens are attempting to have forest areas preserved as pure wilderness, arguing that we should preserve as much of our *natural* (as opposed to manmade) ecology as possible. Preserving wilderness areas involves costs and benefits. The costs include less forest area for other purposes, such as camping grounds and logging. Who bears these costs? People who like to camp (but not backpack) in the first case, and people who buy houses and other wood products,[1] in the second.

Although the reader can easily understand the first case, the second may not be so obvious. Look at it this way. When fewer forest areas are used for logging, then the supply of lumber is smaller than it would be otherwise.[2] With any given demand (schedule) the price of lumber is therefore higher than otherwise. So houses are more expensive.[3]

Now for the benefits. Wilderness-area preservation offers benefits to all those who like backpacking in the preserved area, and all those who can enjoy fishing and hunting there. Benefits are also bestowed upon those who do not themselves backpack, hunt, or fish, but would pay something to keep wilderness for their children.

To determine what effect the saving of a natural ecology area has on the distribution of income broadly defined, we have therefore tried to discover, as always, who bears the costs and who obtains the benefits. This is usually an empirical question which can be answered only by examining relevant data. From limited studies that have been done, we can make a tentative conclusion about wilderness preservation. It has been found that backpackers are, in general, well educated and earn considerably more than the average. Thus the gains from that activity go to middle- and upper-income groups. As for who bears the costs, we know that campers (those with tents, trailers, and camper-trucks) are on average less well-educated than backpackers and earn considerably less. Hence we are trading off recreation facilities used by lower-income people in favor of those used by higher-income people.

As for the increased price of housing due to less lumber, we know that the poor will suffer more than the rich, be-

[1] Or wood-product substitutes, for that matter.
[2] The supply schedule is farther to the left.
[3] Note that the same is also true for nonwood houses. Since the price of wood houses is higher than otherwise, more people substitute nonwood houses—and their price is bid up (their demand schedule shifts outward to the right).

cause housing expenditures are a larger fraction of the poor's budget.

We can easily take other examples. Question: Should the level of a dam be raised to provide more hydroelectric power, or should the virgin timber area around it be left a wilderness area for backpackers? As economists, we cannot answer the question. We can merely point out all of the costs and benefits associated with two (or more) alternatives. In this example the costs (in ecological terms) of raising the dam level would be borne largely by actual and potential backpackers. The benefits would be lower electricity rates and/or the saving of resources that would have been needed to develop an alternative source of energy supply. If electricity payments represent a larger fraction of the income of the poor than the rich, raising the level of the dam might redistribute income from the rich to the poor. We say "might," because the income is redistributed only if the poor pay less relative to what they get.

There is, of course, a way of preserving our ecology without redistributing income.[4] The government could institute user charges for such things as wilderness areas and hunting preserves, setting them to cover the imputed opportunity cost of the resources being used. The totals collected could then be redistributed in a manner that would compensate those bearing the costs.

[4] But not without redistributing the use of resources.

29

THE ECONOMICS
OF INCOME DISTRIBUTION
AND GOVERMENT PROGRAMS

As has been done in many countries, our government has instituted programs for helping sectors of the economy where aid seems to be needed. In most cases the implicit aim of these various programs is to effect a redistribution of income.

As pointed out in the previous chapter, all programs to improve or maintain our environment develop costs and benefits. This is equally true of any other government program. If we are to understand the actual, as opposed to the avowed, redistributional aspects of any governmental policy (or lack of it), we must fully assess the range of costs and benefits. Also we must—once again—determine empirically who bears these costs and benefits.

Let us examine the redistributional effects of the farm program. The obvious intent of this program is to maintain farmers' incomes at a level which society feels is acceptable (that is, not "too" low). The questions to be answered here are: (a) whether in fact the program fulfills that purpose—who bears the benefits; and (b) how the program is paid for—who bears the costs.

To answer the latter question first: All direct and indirect government outlays for the farm program come directly out of government revenues. Taxpayers share in these costs in proportion to the percentage of total receipts they contribute.[1] Direct costs of price supports, surplus storage, and soil banks, added up to $5.6 billion in 1969.

Other costs not directly related to the amount of governmental farm-program expenditure confront the consumer every time he buys a sack of potatoes, in the form of artificially raised prices. It is obvious that the explicit aim of price supports is just that—to support the price of farm crops above what it would have attained under free competition. Comparably, the announced aim of soil banks is "conservation," but one effect is to reduce the supply of cultivated lands and hence the supply of crops offered for sale. To the extent that conservation succeeds, the price of farm products is higher than it would be otherwise. The aim of crop control and marketing quotas is to reduce the supply of the crop that is put onto the market for sale; naturally, the result is again higher prices.

Now, who bears the costs of higher prices? Consumers bear these costs directly, in proportion to the quantity of farm products they buy. It is an empirical fact that the poor spend a larger fraction of their income on food than do the rich.[2] We may, therefore, view the farm programs' resultant higher food prices as a regressive system of taxes which causes a redistribution of the income of the poor, who are actually paying more relative to what they get than the rich.

We have yet to examine who benefits from the farm program. The benefits of higher prices are directly proportional to the amount of farm products sold; therefore, on average,

[1] Taxpayers contribute both directly, via income taxes, and indirectly, via the income they use to buy products for which the prices are higher because their manufacturers also pay taxes.
[2] That is, the income elasticity for food as a whole is less than unity. The German scholar Ernest Engel systematically documented this fact in 1857, and it is now known as Engel's law. As an example, in 1955 nonfarm families with a per capita income of $2,000 spent 27 percent of income on food. Families with per capita income of $600 spent 46 percent.

the benefits are *directly* proportional to a farmer's income.[3] The benefits resulting from governmental buying of "surpluses" are directly proportional to the amount of surpluses sold by a farmer. In general, this indicates that benefits are proportional to farmers' income, since those producing and selling more crops usually derive higher incomes. By the same reasoning, the benefits of the soil-bank program are directly proportional to the number of acres not cultivated. The larger the farm, the larger the amount that can be included in the soil bank and the larger the benefits—which once more are thus positively related to a farmer's income. A few statistics should prove persuasive. About 10 percent of the farmers produce 80–90 percent of the crops marketed. In 1964, farmers earning $100,000 or more received about 60 percent of their total income from direct governmental payments, rent, and dividends. The figure for farmers with incomes of less than $5,000 was a mere 7.7 percent.

After weighing the costs and benefits of our farm program, one can only conclude that its effect is apparently to redistribute income from the poor to the relatively less poor. Of course this assertion could be invalidated if it could be shown that the poor pay proportionately lower taxes toward governmental expenditures than do the rich.

A similar analysis can be applied to the oil-import quota program which results in higher prices for petroleum products. As pointed out before (p. 76), people who earn more than $15,000 spend less than one-half as much of their income on gasoline as do people making less than that figure. The higher price of gasoline due to the quota is therefore

---

[3] Note, though, that if there is free entry into farming, higher prices will induce an increase in the amount of resources devoted to farming. Diminishing returns to incremental factors of production in agriculture insure that in the long run, and with free entry, higher farm prices will not benefit all farmers (unless, of course, the government is buying surpluses and continues to pay for more and more soil banks and the like). With diminishing marginal returns to factors of production, per unit costs rise as output is expanded. Hence high farm prices merely lead to more output until the additional costs of production just match the additional revenue received for the output. At that point, only farmers with specialized talents will be earning more than a normal profit.

an implicit regressive tax, since the poor bear a larger share of these costs, as measured by the proportion of income spent on petroleum products.

On the benefit side, higher prices initially benefit oil producers in direct proportion to the amount of oil sold. In the long run, though, with free entry into the industry, more and more resources will be used until no more than normal competitive profits are earned. The true gainers in the oil-quota program are the stockholders of the companies which are allotted the special import tickets. These tickets have been given out roughly in proportion to the size of the company. The larger the company, the larger the gain. Since the relatively poor in this country own little or no share in these companies (both absolutely and as a percentage of total wealth), this means that the windfall gains go to the rich who experience capital appreciation in their oil-company stocks.

The costs of oil-import quotas (higher gas prices) are borne more by the poor and the gains are reaped by the wealthy. The evident result is a redistribution from the poor to the relatively less poor.

Turning now to our income tax system, let us consider how certain tax deductions redistribute income. A man paying off the mortgage on his home is allowed to deduct the interest payments. This is an incentive for home ownership, since he benefits by not having to apply his marginal tax rate to that amount of income. If a year's mortgage interest payments equal $1,000 and his marginal tax rate is 20 percent, he gains $200 in income that does not have to be handed over to the government. Splendid! But consider now the case of Mr. B., who earns twice the salary and is in the 40 percent tax bracket. For the $2,000 he paid out as interest this year, which he deducts from his income tax, he saves $400. The rich man with a mortgaged home has benefited more than a less rich man in the same situation, and far more than a poor man whose marginal tax rate is zero or than any of those who have no mortgage payments on which to receive concessions.

We have already considered the ways in which income is

redistributed by laws which make abortion, prostitution, and narcotics illegal. Each of the three cases can be summed up by saying that, since information is more costly for illegal goods and services, in general those who can afford to pay more (the wealthy) receive a "better" product than those who are poor.

We can also look back to the questions of rent controls and usury laws. If such laws are effective, they establish a price below the market-clearing one. Dealers in apartments and credit therefore look for nonpecuniary returns when selling their product. Who is a better credit risk, a person who makes $20,000 per year or a person who works off and on for about $5,000 a year? At the same rate of interest, a lender will give funds to the former and not to the latter. The poor get very few loans indeed when usury laws are enforced.

Under rent control, will the landlord rent to a welfare recipient or to the daughter of a city councilman? At the same price, probably to the latter, since she is more likely to make her rent payments regularly.

All of these examples are given to illustrate the need to examine the distribution of the costs and benefits of government programs and to decide whether they actually redistribute income in the intended direction. It appears that many policies tend to favor the rich at the expense of the less rich, but this is an empirical statement which must be verified anew for any prospective program.

30

THE ECONOMICS
OF A NEGATIVE INCOME TAX
AND THE ELIMINATION OF POVERTY

We began this book with Thomas Malthus and a reference to his dismal forecast of man's future. We conclude with a discussion of a proposal which, in effect, would scuttle in the U.S.A. even the residue of the poverty which Malthus expected to be permanently endemic to society. Throughout man's history mass poverty has been accepted as inevitable, and Malthus merely provided a rationale for its inevitability. But the economic growth of the past 200 years in at least a few countries has done away with mass poverty. The poverty that persists is surely not inevitable, but anomalous, in nations of such comparative abundance.

What do we mean by poverty? We must be able to define it if we are going to eliminate it. The Johnson administration offered a set of poverty lines based on an income of $3,000 (in 1959 purchasing power) for a family of four. This figure was then adjusted for variations in family size or, over time, for changes in the value of money. On the strength of this standard, we discover that 32 percent of Americans were poor in 1935, 23 percent in 1959, and that the figure has now fallen to 11 percent.[1] If this trend continues, we shall have eliminated poverty by around 1980. Per capita income has been growing at a real rate of 1.6 percent per year for a long time, and this compound growth rate with no change in income distribution has simply been raising the income level of rich and poor alike. The bottom 20 percent of income receivers have been getting 4 to 5 percent of national income, and this figure has varied little over time.

Although the presently established "poverty line" exceeds the *average* income level in almost every other country in the world, it appears quite clear that we shall not be satisfied with that level even in 1980 and will no doubt raise our sights. When most people think of poverty it is not the absolute level of income that they have in mind, but rather the relative level of income. And this turns out to be a much more stubborn problem to resolve.

The 11 percent of the populace which is poor today is so in spite of a very extensive system of transfer payments which now exists. Old Age, Survivors', Disability, and Health Insurance (OASDHI) payments alone totaled $38 billion in 1968! Unemployment compensation was $2.4 billion. Workmen's compensation was $1.6 billion. All in all total direct payments to people who would have been poorer in the absence of such payments were $48.2 billion, yet the bottom 20 percent of our citizens still received only between 4 and 5 percent of total money income.[2]

What can we do about this? In previous chapters we

[1] We must note that the official figures used today include numerous consumer units that did not exist in former years. The economic unit is not immutable. People seem to demand more independence and privacy as their incomes rise (i.e., there is high income elasticity for these goods). Hence, more economic units are formed, many of them near the "poverty" line because generations in the same family no longer live together as they once did, because more young couples (and old people) are living alone, and because increased divorce rates have added to the number of separate and marginal household units. On the other hand, shifts of population from farms to the city cause us to underestimate poverty, since farm people receive much of their income in the form of home-grown food which is not taken into account.

[2] See Robert J. Lampman, "Transfer Approaches to Distribution Policy," *American Economic Review*, Vol. LX, No. 2 (May 1970), pp. 270–279.

have seen some of the directions that public policy could take. Elementary elimination of discrimination would be a significant step. Maintenance of a full-employment economy would also be a major step because people with few skills have difficulty getting work when there is general unemployment. Educational enrichment and vocational-training programs would clearly contribute to raising income levels of the unskilled. But all of these policies, some of which would take decades to be effective, would still leave a residue of relative poverty. Part of this residue would consist of families and individuals not in the labor force: the aged, the infirm, mothers with small children, etc. Beyond this, some people actually in the labor force would have incomes below the poverty line. In addition, in a dynamic economy there will always be failures in farming and business, frictional unemployment, some large families, and people with limited innate ability or motivation. All these things lead to poverty for those affected.

We can remove this residue of poverty only by giving poor people a claim on others' assets instead of trying to hand them assets directly through increased human-capital investment. In making such a suggestion we are talking, in effect, about a negative income tax.

How would such a program work? Briefly, if it were instituted tomorrow every citizen without exception would fill out an income tax return next April. But for any individual or family whose income fell below the poverty level, the "tax" would be paid *to* him by the United States Treasury instead of taken from him. A most significant point differentiates this program from public assistance or "relief": The taxpayer may *have* income, and still receive the tax benefit as an income supplement necessary to raise his standard of living. He has, in short, an incentive to work. The incentive is directly related to how carefully designed the level of negative tax is. The effective work effort a man or woman puts forth is no doubt related to the rate at which the negative tax benefits fall as earnings rise.

Under the present haphazard jumble of transfer payments, the recipient's usual incentive is not to work, because of the risk of losing his benefits. And the existing programs have added up to many, many billions of dollars while showing no prospect of eliminating the poverty of all the 11 percent of all Americans now classified as poor.

The negative income tax obviously would not do worse and promises to do much better in solving one of the toughest problems facing this country today.[3] A negative income tax is not, however, a panacea. In fact a negative income tax could be devised which most would find totally unacceptable. Every action involves a cost. The fact that negative taxes will destroy some people's incentive to work must be dealt with. Also, there will be a large cost involved in dismantling the present welfare system. Some have maintained that politically and socially it would be easier to modify existing programs. At this point we cannot make a positive statement one way or the other. A leading specialist in this area, Robert J. Lampman, has come up with a price tag that we can all consider in making the decision: It would cost $25 billion a year to eliminate poverty assuming a marginal tax rate of not more than 50 percent and assuming some adjustments in social insurance. The decision is now in the political arena.

[3] *Ibid.*